AMERICA'S DEFENSE
OPPOSING VIEWPOINTS®

Other Books of Related Interest in the Opposing Viewpoints Series:

AMERICA'S DEFENSE
OPPOSING VIEWPOINTS®

David L. Bender & Bruno Leone, *Series Editors*

Carol Wekesser, *Book Editor*

OPPOSING VIEWPOINTS SERIES ®

Greenhaven Press, Inc.   PO Box 289009   San Diego, CA 92198-0009

Library of Congress Cataloging-in-Publication Data

America's defense : opposing viewpoints / Carol Wekesser,
    book editor.
        p.   cm. — (Opposing viewpoints series)
    Includes bibliographical references and index.
    ISBN 0-89908-184-3 (lib) — ISBN 0-89908-159-2 (pap)
    1. United States—Military policy.   2. United States—Armed
    Forces.   I. Wekesser, Carol, 1963-   . II. Series: Opposing
    viewpoints series (Unnumbered)
    UA23.A66328   1991
    355'.0335'73—dc20   91-20163

"Congress shall make no law . . . abridging the freedom of speech, or of the press."

First Amendment to the U.S. Constitution

The basic foundation of our democracy is the first amendment guarantee of freedom of expression. The Opposing Viewpoints Series is dedicated to the concept of this basic freedom and the idea that it is more important to practice it than to enshrine it.

Contents

Why Consider Opposing Viewpoints?

"It is better to debate a question without settling it than to settle a question without debating it."

Joseph Joubert (1754-1824)

The Importance of Examining Opposing Viewpoints

The purpose of the Opposing Viewpoints Series, and this book in particular, is to present balanced, and often difficult to find, opposing points of view on complex and sensitive issues.

Probably the best way to become informed is to analyze the positions of those who are regarded as experts and well studied on issues. It is important to consider every variety of opinion in an attempt to determine the truth. Opinions from the mainstream of society should be examined. But also important are opinions that are considered radical, reactionary, or minority as well as those stigmatized by some other uncomplimentary label. An important lesson of history is the eventual acceptance of many unpopular and even despised opinions. The ideas of Socrates, Jesus, and Galileo are good examples of this.

Readers will approach this book with their own opinions on the issues debated within it. However, to have a good grasp of one's own viewpoint, it is necessary to understand the arguments of those with whom one disagrees. It can be said that those who do not completely understand their adversary's point of view do not fully understand their own.

A persuasive case for considering opposing viewpoints has been presented by John Stuart Mill in his work *On Liberty*. When examining controversial issues it may be helpful to reflect on this suggestion:

The only way in which a human being can make some approach to knowing the whole of a subject, is by hearing what can be said about it by persons of every variety of opinion, and studying all modes in which it can be looked at by every character of mind. No wise man ever acquired his wisdom in any mode but this.

Analyzing Sources of Information

The Opposing Viewpoints Series includes diverse materials taken from magazines, journals, books, and newspapers, as well as statements and position papers from a wide range of individuals, organizations, and governments. This broad spectrum of sources helps to develop patterns of thinking which are open to the consideration of a variety of opinions.

Pitfalls to Avoid

A pitfall to avoid in considering opposing points of view is that of regarding one's own opinion as being common sense and the most rational stance, and the point of view of others as being only opinion and naturally wrong. It may be that another's opinion is correct and one's own is in error.

Another pitfall to avoid is that of closing one's mind to the opinions of those with whom one disagrees. The best way to approach a dialogue is to make one's primary purpose that of understanding the mind and arguments of the other person and not that of enlightening him or her with one's own solutions. More can be learned by listening than speaking.

It is my hope that after reading this book the reader will have a deeper understanding of the issues debated and will appreciate the complexity of even seemingly simple issues on which good and honest people disagree. This awareness is particularly important in a democratic society such as ours where people enter into public debate to determine the common good. Those with whom one disagrees should not necessarily be regarded as enemies, but perhaps simply as people who suggest different paths to a common goal.

Developing Basic Reading and Thinking Skills

In this book, carefully edited opposing viewpoints are purposely placed back to back to create a running debate; each viewpoint is preceded by a short quotation that best expresses the author's main argument. This format instantly plunges the reader into the midst of a controversial issue and greatly aids that reader in mastering the basic skill of recognizing an author's point of view.

A number of basic skills for critical thinking are practiced in the activities that appear throughout the books in the series. Some of the skills are:

Evaluating Sources of Information. The ability to choose from among alternative sources the most reliable and accurate source in relation to a given subject.

Separating Fact from Opinion. The ability to make the basic distinction between factual statements (those that can be demonstrated or verified empirically) and statements of opinion (those that are beliefs or attitudes that cannot be proved).

Identifying Stereotypes. The ability to identify oversimplified, exaggerated descriptions (favorable or unfavorable) about people and insulting statements about racial, religious, or national groups, based upon misinformation or lack of information.

Recognizing Ethnocentrism. The ability to recognize attitudes or opinions that express the view that one's own race, culture, or group is inherently superior, or those attitudes that judge another culture or group in terms of one's own.

It is important to consider opposing viewpoints and equally important to be able to critically analyze those viewpoints. The activities in this book are designed to help the reader master these thinking skills. Statements are taken from the book's viewpoints and the reader is asked to analyze them. This technique aids the reader in developing skills that not only can be applied to the viewpoints in this book, but also to situations where opinionated spokespersons comment on controversial issues. Although the activities are helpful to the solitary reader, they are most useful when the reader can benefit from the interaction of group discussion.

Using this book and others in the series should help readers develop basic reading and thinking skills. These skills should improve the reader's ability to understand what is read. Readers should be better able to separate fact from opinion, substance from rhetoric, and become better consumers of information in our media-centered culture.

This volume of the Opposing Viewpoints Series does not advocate a particular point of view. Quite the contrary! The very nature of the book leaves it to the reader to formulate the opinions he or she finds most suitable. My purpose as publisher is to see that this is made possible by offering a wide range of viewpoints that are fairly presented.

David L. Bender
Publisher

Introduction

"The United States has emerged from this war in a position of undisputed military power."

—*Insight*, March 25, 1991.

"The Gulf War is dangerous because it played up the efficacy and even glamour of military remedies for foreign policy headaches."

—*The Washington Monthly*, April 1991.

In 1973, the United States pulled its last remaining troops out of Vietnam. While this officially ended American military involvement in Southeast Asia, it did not end the devastating impact the war had on Americans. The U.S. withdrawal from Vietnam marked the end of a failed policy of military intervention that had divided the nation politically and emotionally. Americans had begun to doubt not only the wisdom and morality of such intervention, but the strength of the nation as well. As *Time* magazine writer Stanley W. Cloud states, "The pain of . . . Vietnam memories . . . somehow only increased as the years passed." The failure in Vietnam caused "a national trauma concerning the use of military force," according to columnist William Pfaff.

These feelings of defeat and moral uncertainty lasted from the war's end until 1991, when the U.S. led international troops to defeat Iraq. The majority of Americans supported U.S. involvement in the Gulf, believing it to be a moral and necessary use of America's military. They felt vindicated after the U.S. and Allied forces' swift and decisive victory. The misgivings of Vietnam gave way to confidence and enthusiasm. "By God, we've kicked the Vietnam syndrome once and for all," declared President George Bush. "Operation Desert Storm is proof positive that the American military is not hobbled by a 'Vietnam syndrome,'" concluded Harry G. Summers Jr., retired U.S. Army colonel and a Distinguished Fellow of the Army War College. A 1991 *USA Today* poll found that 78 percent of Americans had "a great deal of confidence in the military," compared with 23 percent in 1977.

How this new-found confidence will affect the future of the nation and its armed forces, however, remains controversial. Will the victory in the Gulf lead to a renewed enthusiasm for solving conflicts using force, perhaps dooming the U.S. to yet another Vietnam-like conflict? Or has America learned enough from its experiences in Vietnam and the Gulf to choose its battles carefully and judiciously? *America's Defense: Opposing Viewpoints* examines the effectiveness and the future of the armed forces. The following chapters are included: What Role Should the U.S. Play in World Defense? Should Women Serve in the U.S. Military? Should Defense Spending Be Decreased? and What Weapons Would Strengthen America's Defense? As the events of the Persian Gulf War are assessed, rehashed, and debated, they provide Americans with an opportunity to examine the issues related to America's defense.

What Role Should the U.S. Play in World Defense?

AMERICA'S DEFENSE

Chapter Preface

For nearly forty-five years, the purpose of America's military was to deter Soviet aggression and the spread of communism throughout the world. To this end, the U.S. provided military aid and sometimes troops to countries in Central America, Africa, Asia, Europe, and the Middle East. Decreased U.S.-Soviet tensions and the decreasing threat of communism to world peace, however, have forced the U.S. to reevaluate this military goal. Many experts believe that the absence of a Soviet threat is justification for reducing America's military forces. Others have interpreted the war with Iraq and threats from other unstable regions to mean that the U.S. should continue its prominent military role in the world.

Those who support reduced military involvement argue that after years of being "the world's policeman," it is now time for the U.S. to rely more on diplomacy and less on military strength. In fact, many analysts believe that rather than protecting weaker nations from the Soviet threat, U.S. military involvement merely increased political tensions in those countries. For example, many of these analysts believe that by supplying the Nicaraguan contras with arms, the U.S. lengthened Nicaragua's ten-year civil war, increasing the bloodshed and political and economic instability. Reducing America's military role would reduce the likelihood of the U.S. becoming involved in future Nicaraguas. As Cato Institute director Ted Galen Carpenter states, "Not only does the United States no longer have to police the planet," but this reduced role will prevent it from "intruding on the interests of other powers, thereby creating needless frictions and confrontations."

Those who argue that America should continue its prominent role in the world maintain that it is vital, perhaps now more than ever, for the United States to continue to be the world's dominant military power. Regional conflicts and political instability in the Middle East, Eastern Europe, and Latin America still necessitate American military involvement to protect the interests of the U.S. and its allies and to protect weaker nations such as Kuwait from aggressors such as Iraq. "Although the heated superpower rivalry has cooled, the likelihood of crises of other sorts has increased, as deep-seated and long-repressed disputes have revived and potential new conflicts have emerged," writes Michael D. Rich, a Rand Corporation scholar. "The United States will continue to stand above all other nations in its global military reach and overall influence. . . . Thus, it will have to take a leading role in the creation of a new world security order," Rich concludes.

For many years, the primary role of the U.S. military was to deter Soviet aggression. With that goal decreasing in importance, the U.S. must now reflect on what role its military should play in world affairs. That role is the focus of the debates presented in the following chapter.

VIEWPOINT

1

"The world is still a dangerous place and the United States must continue to play the leading role on the world's stage."

The U.S. Must Maintain a Strong Military Role in World Affairs

Richard Nixon

The United States is the world's leading military power, and it must continue to play a strong military role in world affairs, Richard Nixon argues in the following viewpoint. Nixon believes that the U.S. needs a strong military to protect its interests throughout the world and to deter potential Soviet and German aggression in Europe and Soviet, Chinese, and Japanese aggression in Asia. Nixon was president of the United States from 1969 to 1974. Since the end of his presidency, Nixon has been a foreign policy advisor to several U.S. presidents and has written many books, including *In the Arena: A Memoir of Victory, Defeat, and Renewal*, and *1999: The Global Challenges We Face in the Next Decade*.

As you read, consider the following questions:

1. Why does Nixon believe the U.S. war with Iraq was justified?
2. What evidence does the author give to support his contention that the U.S. is the world's only complete superpower?
3. What does Nixon believe is the most important challenge facing the U.S.?

Richard Nixon, "A War About Peace," *European Affairs*, February/March 1991. Reprinted with permission.

Some liberal pundits and politicians have criticized US Senate Republican leader Bob Dole for saying that the US sent its forces to the Persian Gulf for oil and Secretary of State Jim Baker for saying that we went there to protect jobs. There are more important reasons, but let us not be so hypocritical as to say that preventing an international outlaw from controlling 40% of the world's oil reserves is not a critical interest of the United States and a justifiable reason for sending forces to the Gulf. Let us suppose that instead of Kuwait this had been Nepal, or Upper Volta, or Paraguay being gobbled up by a neighboring state. Does anyone seriously suggest that we would have sent in the Marines to liberate them?

Not a Fight for Democracy

It is equally hypocritical to contend that we are there in support of democracy. None of our Arab allies are democracies and putting the Emir of Kuwait back in power is not going to bring democracy to the Kuwaiti people.

And it is not enough to justify our sending armed forces to the Gulf because Saddam Hussein happens to be a cruel leader. President Bush has been criticized for equating him with Hitler. Whether he is that bad is irrelevant. He is bad enough. His army raped, looted and murdered the defenseless people of Kuwait. He held thousands of hostages as human shields. To praise him for releasing hostages he should not have taken in the first place is ludicrous. He has a history of violating international law by using chemical weapons. If the aim of the US in the Gulf were to punish cruel leaders, we would not be allied with Syrian President Assad, who ordered the massacre of 20,000 innocent men, women and children in the city of Hama in his own country, who has supported international terrorism and possibly the bombing of civilian aircraft, and whose troops have committed brutal atrocities in his campaign to dominate Lebanon.

The US went to the Gulf for two major reasons. Saddam Hussein had unlimited ambitions to dominate one of the most important strategic areas in the world. Because he had oil, he had the means to acquire the weapons he needed for aggression against his neighbors, including at some future time a nuclear arsenal. If he had succeeded in Kuwait, he would have attacked others and would use whatever weapons he had, including chemical and nuclear, to achieve his goals. If we did not stop him now, we would have to stop him later when the cost in the lives of young Americans would have been infinitely greater. We had to use force as approved by the United Nations resolution. War is bad, but a bad peace is worse because it can lead to a bigger war.

There is an even more important long-term reason for turning back his aggression. The whole world is heaving a collective sigh of relief as the Cold War appears to be coming to an end. Many believe that we are entering a new era where armed aggression will no longer be an instrument of national policy. We can't be sure that their hopes will be justified. But we can be sure that if Saddam Hussein had gained from his aggression against Kuwait, there are other potential aggressors in the world who would have been tempted to wage war against their neighbors. If we fail to roll back this kind of aggression, no potential aggressor in the future will be deterred by warnings from the United States or by UN resolutions. Getting him out of Kuwait and eliminating his capacity to wage aggressive war in the future gives the US the credibility to deter aggression elsewhere without sending in American armed forces because potential aggressors will know that when the United States warns against aggression we have the means and the will to back up our warnings. . . .

Facing the Problem

Americans tend to think of international relations in engineering terms: A set of "problems" that need to be "solved" so that they can be promptly forgotten. With the end of the Cold War, it would be nice if our future were one in which many powers of comparable weight would balance each other off and produce a peaceful world. Then we could turn fully to our pressing domestic economic, educational, environmental and social welfare agenda. But international relations is not a set of "problems to be solved" but rather a set of "conditions to be managed." If we do not face up to these conditions, and if we once again turn inward, others will come forward to assert their military power and none of us will be better off as a result.

Michael Nacht, *The Washington Post National Weekly Edition,* April 23-29, 1990.

Forty-four years ago in his Iron Curtain speech in Fulton, Missouri, Winston Churchill said, "The United States stands at the pinnacle of world power. This is a solemn moment for the American democracy. For with primacy in power is joined an awe-inspiring accountability for the future."

Those words are as true today as they were then. The Soviet threat has declined but as the crisis in the Gulf demonstrates the world is still a dangerous place and the United States must continue to play the leading role on the world's stage—not as a world policeman but in conflicts like the Gulf where our vital interests are involved. We have to play that role because there is no one else to take our place—not the British, not the French, not the Russians, not the Japanese, and despite some woolly-headed dreaming to the contrary, not the United Nations.

Some question whether we are able to play that role. It is fashionable in some academic circles to say that the United States, like the Soviet Union, is in decline and no longer has the means to play a leading role on the world's stage.

Some Awesome Problems

The US has some awesome problems—drugs, crime, the urban underclass, the deficit. But before World War II the United States produced 24% of the world's GNP [gross national product]. Today it produces 26% and by the end of the century it will be 28%—two-and-one-half times as much as Japan and five times as much as a united Germany.

The United States today is the world's only complete super-power—economic, military and political. As economist Herb Stein has pointed out, "The United States is a very rich country—not rich enough to do everything but rich enough to do everything important."

There is a major new factor, however, since Churchill spoke those words in 1946. For 45 years after the end of World War II, the United States has carried the major burden of foreign aid, including aid to Japan and Germany, who are now our major economic competitors. It is time for other rich countries like Japan and the nations of Western Europe to assume the major portion of that burden since our military power still protects them as well as ourselves. For example, Japan gets 66% of its oil from the Gulf. The US gets 10% of its oil from the Gulf.

However, the US should continue to shoulder its other major burdens and responsibilities. We are witnessing the unusual phenomenon of isolationists on the right and left, urging that since the Cold War is over, we should withdraw all of our forces from Europe, particularly since the nations of Europe have recovered from the devastation of World War II and should be able to provide for their own defense.

But what would Europe be without an American military presence? Great Britain and France are minor nuclear powers. Germany is an economic superpower without nuclear weapons. The Soviet Union even without Eastern Europe will still be a nuclear superpower with the world's largest conventional army. No one can seriously suggest that the British and French would use their nuclear forces to deter a Soviet attack on Germany. With US forces gone from Europe and NATO [North Atlantic Treaty Organization] dissolved, Germany would have the option of going nuclear or neutral and would be strongly tempted to become a political and economic ally of the Soviet Union. Either of these options is bad for Europe, bad for Germany, and bad for the United States.

We can and should cut our NATO forces substantially because of the dissolution of the Warsaw Pact. But a significant conventional and nuclear US presence in Europe is necessary as insurance against a possible renewal of the Soviet threat and as reassurance for those who fear a resurgent German threat. I do not share the concern that a united Germany would again become an aggressive military power. But despite their public statements, many European leaders have that concern.

The U.S. in Asia

Conservative and liberal isolationists say that because there is no longer a Soviet threat in Asia, we should bring our forces home from Japan and Korea, particularly since they are now rich enough to defend themselves. They are wrong. Keeping an American military presence in Europe is important. Keeping one in Asia is indispensable if we are to have peace in the Pacific. Let us look at Asia without the United States:

- The Soviet Union, a nuclear superpower that while reducing its forces in Europe has strengthened its naval and nuclear forces in Asia.
- China, which will be a nuclear superpower within 10 to 20 years.
- Japan, an economic superpower without nuclear weapons and without a US defense guarantee. Japan would have no choice but to go nuclear or to make a deal with the strongest of its neighbors, the Soviet Union. Japan can afford to massively increase its defense forces. But even more than is the case with Germany's neighbors in Europe, the Japanese in Asia are feared by the Koreans, the Chinese, the Filipinos, the Taiwanese, the Malaysians and the Indonesians, all of whom suffered from Japanese occupation in World War II. A US military presence in Japan and Korea is indispensable if we are to preserve peace in the Pacific.

Look at China. We should continue to deplore the tragedy of Tiananmen Square. But the Bush administration is right to restore diplomatic and economic cooperation with the PRC [People's Republic of China]. This is in our interest and in the interest of the Chinese people. It is in our interest because China has a veto in the UN Security Council and plays an indispensable role in trying to resolve the continuing conflicts in Southeast Asia. And in the non-military area, how can we possibly have a coordinated international initiative on problems of environment with one-fifth of the world's people not cooperating?

The restoration of a cooperative relationship between China and the United States is without question in the interest of human rights for the Chinese people. China is not a democracy and will not become one in the foreseeable future. But as we saw in Korea and Taiwan, economic progress inevitably leads to political progress. Economic cooperation, tourism, Chinese students studying in the United States will strengthen the prospects for political reform. That is why Secretary Baker was following the right course in meeting with the Chinese Foreign Minister and why the administration was justified in supporting the resumption of World Bank loans to China. For the United States to continue to isolate China economically and diplomatically only strengthens the hardliners in China. The only hope for political reform is to reestablish the cooperative relationship we had with China before the tragic events at Tiananmen. . . .

America's Role

Communism has been rejected because it didn't work. Freedom is now on trial: Will freedom provide the economic and political progress the communists promised and did not produce? Democracy and freedom do not automatically produce progress. Look at the enormous problems in the new democracies in Eastern Europe and the problems in Brazil and Argentina, countries that are trying to make the painful transition from command to free-market economies.

The United States is the oldest and most successful democracy in the world. Our challenge is to provide an example for others to follow. Our challenge is to make the twenty-first century a century of peace and to leave as our legacy not just the defeat of communism and fascism but the victory of freedom.

2 VIEWPOINT

"The U.S. should . . . reduce its foreign military involvements."

The U.S. Should Reduce Its Military Role in World Affairs

Center for Defense Information

The Center for Defense Information is a Washington, D.C., organization that opposes excessive defense spending and U.S. military intervention. In the following viewpoint, the author proposes that the U.S. decrease its military involvement in other countries. The author supports this proposal by arguing that military involvement does not benefit the U.S. and does nothing to preserve world peace.

As you read, consider the following questions:

1. What nonmilitary threats face the U.S., according to the author?
2. How has the importance of military power changed, in the author's opinion?
3. Why does the author believe that Germany and Japan no longer pose a threat to world peace?

Center for Defense Information, *The U.S. as the World's Policeman? Ten Reasons to Find a Different Role,* vol. 20, no. 1, 1991. Reprinted with permission.

Under the Bush Administration, the United States appears to be expanding the role it has long performed as global policeman. President Bush's vision of a "new world order" seems to mean that the U.S. military's mission is shifting from "fighting communism" to capturing drug lords and stopping dictators. It is shifting from defending half the world against the other half to defending the entire world against new "threats" sometimes identified by the Pentagon simply as "instability, uncertainty, and unpredictability."

The Persian Gulf

Since August 1990, President Bush has assembled a military force of about 460,000 U.S. troops in the Middle East to do battle with Iraq and Saddam Hussein. After the war in the Persian Gulf ends, the Bush Administration may seek to maintain American military personnel in Saudi Arabia or on the territory of other countries in the Middle East on a long-term basis. These forces would join almost half a million U.S. troops—one quarter of all active-duty American men and women in uniform—already stationed on military bases in foreign countries and aboard ships in distant waters.

With the U.S. military buildup in the Persian Gulf, 40 percent of all active-duty American military personnel [were] deployed outside the U.S. and its territorial waters. Prior to the Gulf conflict, 435,000 U.S. troops already were assigned to 395 major military bases in 35 foreign countries. Accompanying them were more than 168,000 civilian Pentagon employees and 400,000 family dependents. Another 47,000 U.S. Navy and Marine Corps personnel were stationed aboard ships in foreign waters and 10,000 U.S. troops were stationed at 20 military bases on the American overseas territorial possessions of Guam, Johnston Atoll, the Marshall Islands, Midway Island, Puerto Rico, the Virgin Islands, and Wake Island.

Altogether, today more than a million American military personnel and civilian Pentagon employees are stationed abroad. Prior to World War II, the U.S. maintained only a handful of military installations in foreign countries. When troops were dispatched overseas they generally were returned home in short order. The first permanent U.S. bases in foreign countries were established in Cuba and in the Philippines following the Spanish-American War in 1898.

After World War II, America adopted a strategy of "forward defense" to contain perceived Soviet expansionism by establishing "front lines" at outposts far from U.S. shores. Today the danger posed by the Soviet Union has receded. The containment mission upon which forward defense rested has essentially disappeared. Yet the Bush Administration is busy finding new rationales to keep American troops stationed in distant corners of the world in perpetuity.

In the 1980s the U.S. annually spent about $160-$170 billion to defend countries in Europe, $30-$40 billion to defend countries in Asia, and $20-$40 billion to protect U.S. access to Persian Gulf oil. This included the costs of pay, operations, maintenance, training, and support for American military forces based in foreign countries and for all planned reinforcements from the U.S., plus the costs of the research, development, and production of weapons and other equipment used by these forces.

Reprinted by permission: Tribune Media Services.

Future U.S. military spending must be weighed against growing nonmilitary threats to American security not included in Pentagon "threat scenarios." These include a deepening budget crunch, trade deficits, a $3 trillion national debt, inadequate health care, drug problems, homelessness, deteriorating highways and bridges, a $500 billion savings-and-loan bailout, and perhaps as much as $300 billion worth of damage to the environment from operations at Pentagon bases and Department of Energy nuclear weapons plants.

In the post-Cold War world the U.S. should now be able to meet critical domestic needs while still satisfying all essential security requirements. It can reduce its annual military budget to two-thirds or less of its present size. It can cut its nuclear forces by three quarters and its conventional forces by one half. The U.S. can safely reduce by almost a million the number of its active-duty military personnel. These reductions should begin with troops in Europe, Japan, South Korea, and the Philippines. . . .

Reasons for Reductions

There are at least 6 good reasons why the U.S. should begin gradually to reduce its foreign military involvements, close down its costly foreign bases, and withdraw and demobilize all U.S. troops in foreign countries by the year 2000.

Reason 1: U.S. military forces based in foreign countries do not contribute to the defense of the U.S. There is no national consensus about what constitutes the "vital interests" of the U.S. There is also no consensus about how to protect them. Interests change with time and politics, but most people would agree that America does not have interests everywhere in the world and that some interests matter more than others.

According to General Wallace Nutting, former Commander-in-Chief of the U.S. Readiness Command, "We today do not have a single soldier, airman, or sailor solely dedicated to the security mission within the United States." In fact, about 70 percent of America's annual military spending and most of its military forces—even those based in the U.S.—are intended to further U.S. capabilities for fighting nonnuclear, "conventional" wars in foreign countries. . . .

Interests that were defined in the context of the Cold War—particularly containment of communism—are now overdue for reevaluation. Those interests precious enough to be deemed "vital interests" should have a direct, immediate, and substantial connection with America's physical survival. First and foremost the U.S. should defend its own territory and the immediate approaches to its territory.

Reason 2: The U.S. is not bound by treaties to use its military forces to defend other countries. Two hundred years ago George Washington admonished his countrymen to "steer clear of permanent alliances." Thomas Jefferson spoke of "peace, commerce, and honest friendship with all nations, entangling alliances with none." For most of America's history their advice was heeded. Since World War II, however, the U.S. has signed military treaties with 43 countries.

Nevertheless, not one U.S. defense treaty with other countries commits America to military action in the event of an attack on its treaty partners. Nor does any treaty require the U.S. to station its armed forces on another country's territory. . . .

Reason 3: The world has changed significantly. The existing U.S. military force structure, with its forward deployment of troops and weapons in foreign countries and waters, was designed to meet the perceived threats of a very different world. Over the past few years some startling changes have taken place.

Communism in Eastern Europe has collapsed. East and West Germany have united. As a military organization the Warsaw Pact is defunct. It is expected that Soviet military forces will empty out of Czechoslovakia and Hungary completely by mid-1991, Poland perhaps by 1992, and Germany by 1994. The Soviets also are reducing their forces in Asia and have declared their intention to withdraw all of their foreign-based troops by the year 2000.

Just how much the world has changed is perhaps most evident in Germany's agreement to pay the Soviet Union several billion dollars a year to subsidize—until they depart—the 600,000 Soviet troops and dependents remaining in what used to be East Germany. In Asia, meanwhile, the Soviet Union may return several islands to Japan which it has occupied since World War II. Relations between North and South Korea are improving to the point where federation before the end of the century seems possible.

The Waning Importance of Military Power

In today's world national power has become more complex. It is defined as much by economic, social, and political components as by military power. Today military power generally is less practical, less usable, and less translatable into political or economic advantage. Increasingly, economic leadership is the true measure of a nation's strength. While governments in the Soviet Union, Europe, and Japan appear to have recognized this, U.S. officials lag behind.

America can ill afford to continue to postpone putting its economic house in order. It needs an economy that is innovative, that is dynamic, and that is doing the kinds of things people now see Japan doing. If the economic challenge goes unmet, then our security is threatened. The American way of life can be endangered by economic weakness just as surely as by a Soviet attack. In fact, economic vulnerability now is a much greater threat to the U.S. than Soviet aggression.

Reason 4: Other countries are capable of providing their own defenses. The countries hosting U.S. troops are more than capable of providing for themselves whatever military forces they deem necessary. Europe and Japan have long since recovered from the ravages of World War II. If anything, the ongoing U.S. military subsidy only acts as an incentive for host countries to be militarily weak, perpetuates a dependent relationship, and suggests that the security of these countries means more to the U.S. than it does to them.

Today the European members of the NATO [North Atlantic Treaty Organization] military alliance have a collective gross national product (GNP) greater than that of the U.S. and at least two times greater than that of the Soviet Union. Yet America spends more on NATO defenses than the other 15 alliance members combined.

America's European NATO allies collectively have more than 3 million active-duty troops drawn from a combined population of almost 400 million. If needed, between them there are 87 million males aged 15-49 available for military service. Excluding Britain and Iceland, neither of which has compulsory military service, about 2.6 million males in the remaining 12 European NATO countries reach draft age annually.

Plenty of Weapons

Beyond questions of manpower sufficiency, France, Britain, Germany, and Italy—powerful industrial countries that are among the world's 10 leading exporters of weapons—are capable of manufacturing in mass quantity all of the weapons necessary to satisfy their own security requirements. France and Britain also possess sizable stocks of nuclear weapons. . . .

Reason 5: The world does not need the U.S. to be global policeman. The Bush Administration maintains that American troops must remain in allied countries as their security blanket, preparing not only to meet every known threat and enemy, but also to meet the "unforeseeable," and as yet unidentified, threats and enemies that may or may not materialize in the future. It cautions that the U.S. must guard against a possible reversal of policy in the Soviet Union and serve as a stabilizing force in the face of potential "volatility" and "turbulence" from ethnic, nationality, and religious conflicts and separatist movements.

CIA [Central Intelligence Agency] director William Webster, however, advised Congress in early 1990 that "even if a hardline regime were able to retain power in Moscow, it would have little incentive to engage in major confrontations with the United States." Defense Secretary Richard Cheney acknowledged, "The threat of a sudden attack by Soviet forces in Europe has basically evaporated." And General Colin Powell, chairman of the Joint Chiefs of Staff, stated, "In the Pacific it is unlikely that the Soviets would initiate hostilities which threaten our interests."

With the November 1990 signing of the Conventional Forces in Europe (CFE) Treaty, the Soviet Union has agreed to destroy tens of thousands of its tanks, armored combat vehicles, artillery weapons, and combat aircraft. In the future the U.S. may have as much as 2 years' warning in which to dispatch military forces to Europe in the unlikely event that the Soviet military decided to prepare to fight its way through Eastern Europe to attack Western Europe.

No Need for U.S. Involvement

Many uncertainties and potential instabilities in the world are either peripheral or irrelevant to U.S. security and thus do not warrant American military involvement. If Romania and Hungary were to go to war over the disputed territory of Transylvania, for example, or if hostilities between Croatia and Serbia were to lead to civil war in Yugoslavia, in neither case would vital American interests be threatened.

The U.N. Security Council, with its multinational peace-keeping forces, or the strengthened dispute resolution mechanisms of the Conference on Security and Cooperation in Europe (CSCE), including the newly established Center for the Prevention of Conflict, are better suited to intervene in such situations than are U.S. troops.

Increasingly, the leading concerns of nations in Western Europe are drugs, unemployment, environmental degradation, and the potential mass immigration of people from Eastern Europe and elsewhere—hardly problems that can be prevented or resolved with U.S. military forces. Military might is a blunt instrument good at destroying things and killing people, but not at resolving complex political, ethnic, religious, and historical disputes.

It is not in America's interest to be the world's "911 number." If the U.S. withdraws its forward-based military forces, the world is not going to come apart and America's security is not going to suffer. Since the peak years of the 1960s when it had bases in or special access arrangements with more than 60 countries, the U.S. has pulled military forces out of a number of countries. In no case has this led to a lasting decline in security. . . .

Reason 6: U.S. military forces are not needed to deter German and Japanese rearmament. The reason for stationing U.S. military forces in Europe and in Asia sometimes has been expressed as follows: "to keep the Soviets out, the Americans in, and the Germans and Japanese down." Pointing to the last objective, some argue that withdrawing U.S. military forces would leave "power vacuums" that would encourage former World War II villains Germany and Japan to rearm even more than they already have, making neighboring countries apprehensive and resulting in regional instability.

Even while American troops have been stationed on their soil both countries, with U.S. encouragement, have amassed powerful militaries. Continuing to keep U.S. troops in Germany and Japan will not prevent these countries from exercising their sovereign right to further add to their armed forces if they so choose. On the other hand, it should be recognized that German and Japanese citizens today have thoroughly rejected militarism and aggression. . . .

Whither the U.S.?

The Pentagon's "forward defense" strategy of stationing U.S. military forces in foreign countries and in distant waters is now obsolete. America far too long has born the burden of defending other countries that now are more than capable of defending themselves.

The U.S. has a choice. It can adapt to a changing world and begin drastically to reduce its military burdens by closing its foreign military bases and bringing troops home. We can choose to pay greater attention to crucial nonmilitary determinants of the nation's security—social, political, economic, and environmental components. Or, the U.S. can further strain its economy and weaken its security by continuing and expanding its role as the world's policeman.

"Militarily significant U.S. forces must remain on the other side of the Atlantic for as long as our allies want—and need—them."

The U.S. Must Continue to Defend Europe

George Bush

Although the Soviet threat to Europe has decreased dramatically, the U.S. should maintain its commitment to defend Europe, George Bush argues in the following viewpoint. Bush maintains that because the outcome of Soviet reforms is still uncertain, the U.S. and its NATO allies must remain unified and prepared to defend Europe. An American military presence protected the peace in Europe for forty-five years, Bush states, and can continue to promote stability in the region. Bush was elected president of the United States in 1988.

As you read, consider the following questions:

1. What four points should NATO leaders address concerning European security, in the author's opinion?
2. What changes does Bush plan to make concerning nuclear weapons in Europe?
3. Why does Bush want to strengthen the role of the Conference on Security and Cooperation in Europe?

George Bush, "NATO and the U.S. Commitment to Europe," *U.S. Department of State Dispatch,* September 3, 1990. Public Domain.

Postwar America was ready for peace and prosperity. But while the free world was recovering, the nations of Eastern Europe were being "consolidated" behind an Iron Curtain. So began four decades of division in Europe—and 40 long years of suspicion between superpowers.

Today, [we are witnessing] the end of an era of conflict—but a contest of a different kind, a cold and abstract war of words and walls. Now Europe and the world have entered a new era, the "age of freedom.". . .

Throughout our history, great upheavals in Europe have forced the American people to respond, to make deep judgments about the part we should play in European affairs. This has been true from the time of the French Revolution and the wars which followed it; to World War I and the flawed peace which ended it; to the Second World War and the creation of the postwar order. I believe that, now, we are poised at another such moment—a critical time in our strategic relationship with our neighbors across the Atlantic.

Many of the graduates of America's class of 1916 may have wondered why the faraway war making headlines in their newspapers would have anything to do with them. They might have agreed with President Woodrow Wilson, who that year said, "We are not interested" in the causes of war, in "the obscure foundations from which its stupendous flood has burst forth." But a year later, those classmates—and their country —were swept up in the torrent, carrying them to the horror of the trenches in France.

Yet after the war, we again turned away from active involvement in European affairs. Instead, we sponsored a treaty to outlaw war, and then, as the outlaws gained strength, the United States passed new neutrality laws. Another generation of Americans sat in the bright sun of commencement ceremonies at colleges across the country, thinking war in Europe would pass them by. But when war came, they paid an awful price for America's isolation.

When that war ended, those students no longer questioned our role in the future of Europe. They no longer asked what Europe had to do with them, because they knew the answer: everything.

About a year ago in Germany, I defined the kind of Europe our country is committed to: a peaceful, stable Europe, a Europe whole and free. Today that goal is within our reach.

A New Age of Freedom

We are entering a new "age of freedom" in a time of uncertainty but great hope. Emerging democracies in Eastern Europe are going through social, political, and economic transformations; shaking loose stagnant, centralized bureaucracies that have smothered initiative for generations.

In this time of transition, moving away from the postwar era and beyond containment, we cannot know what choices the people of Eastern Europe will make for their future. The process of change in the Soviet Union is also still unfinished. It will be crucial to see, for example, whether Moscow chooses coercion or peaceful dialogue in responding to the aspirations of the Lithuanian people, and [other] nationalities within the Soviet Union. The only noble answer lies in a dialogue that results in unencumbered self-determination for Lithuania.

A Commitment to Europe

The criteria for the U.S. security relationship with Europe are clear. The American people need to feel committed to Europe in terms that will convince Europeans that, if need be, U.S. power will be returned to the continent. Not surprisingly, these were also the criteria for U.S. engagement during the past 40 years. Given the profound changes taking place in Europe, especially in Soviet power and ambition, it should in fact be easier for the United States to play a useful role as a European power in the future than it did, successfully, in the past.

Robert E. Hunter, *The Washington Quarterly,* Autumn 1990.

President Mikhail Gorbachev has made profound progress in his country; reforms so fundamental that the clock cannot be turned back. Yet, neither can we turn the clock ahead, to know for sure what kind of country the Soviet Union will be in years to come. For the sake of the future we share with Europe, our policies and presence must be appropriate for this period of transition—with a constancy and reliability that will reassure our friends, both old and new.

My European colleagues want the United States to be a part of Europe's future. I believe they are right. The United States should remain a European power in the broadest sense—politically, militarily, and economically. And, as part of our global responsibilities, the foundation for America's peaceful engagement in Europe has been—and will continue to be—NATO [North Atlantic Treaty Organization].

Recognizing in peace what we had learned from war, we joined with the free nations of Europe to form an Atlantic community, an enduring political compact. Our engagement in Europe has meant that the Europeans accept America as part of their continent's future, taking our interests into account across the board. Our commitment is not just in defense; it must be a well-bal-

33

anced mix of involvement in all dimensions of European affairs.

Because of our political commitment to peace in Europe, there has not been a war on that continent in 45 years. This "long peace" should be viewed through the long lens of history: Europe has now experienced the longest uninterrupted period of international peace in the recorded history of that continent. The alliance is now ready to build on that historic achievement and define its objectives for the next century. So the alliance must join together to craft a new Western strategy for new and changing times. . . .

Margaret Thatcher, one of freedom's greatest champions of the last decade, told me that while NATO has been fantastically successful, we should be ready now to face new challenges. The time is right for the alliance to act. . . .

To my NATO colleagues, I suggest that [we] address four critical points:

> One, the political role NATO can play in the new Europe.
> Two, the conventional forces the alliance will need in the time ahead, and NATO's goals for conventional arms control.
> Three, the role of nuclear weapons based in Europe—and Western objectives in new nuclear arms control negotiations between the US and the Soviet Union.
> Four, strengthening the Conference on Security and Cooperation in Europe—the CSCE—to reinforce NATO and help protect democratic values, in a Europe whole and free.

The first task the NATO [leaders] should consider is the future political mission of the alliance. As military threats fade, the political dimension of NATO's work—always there, but seldom noticed—becomes more prominent. So . . . we should look for ways to help our German friends sustain freedom and achieve unity—something which we and our allies have supported for over 40 years. And, we should reaffirm the importance of keeping a united Germany a full member of NATO.

The alliance needs to find ways to work more closely with a vigorous European Community that is rightly asserting its own distinct views. And in Eastern Europe, governments once our adversaries are now our partners in building a new continent. So we must also talk about how to encourage further peaceful democratic change in Eastern Europe and in the Soviet Union.

But even as NATO gives more emphasis to its political mission, its guarantee of European security must remain firm. Our enemy today is uncertainty and instability, so the alliance will need to maintain a sound, collective military structure with forces in the field, backed by larger forces that can be called upon in a crisis.

Which brings me to the second task for NATO [leaders]—a review of how the alliance should plan its conventional defenses.

While we need to recognize that it will take some time before the Soviet military presence is gone from Eastern Europe—and before the major reductions contemplated by both sides can be implemented—we need to develop our strategy for that world now.

Obviously, Soviet actions will be critical. Yet even after all the planned reductions in its forces are complete—even if our current arms control proposals are agreed to and implemented—the Soviet military will still field forces, dwarfing those of any other single European state, armed with thousands of nuclear weapons. Militarily significant US forces must remain on the other side of the Atlantic for as long as our allies want—and need —them. These forces demonstrate, as no words can, the enduring political compact that binds America's fate with Europe's democracies.

If the Soviet withdrawal continues and our arms control efforts are successful, we must plan for a different kind of military presence focused less on the danger of an immediate outbreak of war. We must promote long-term stability and prevent crises from escalating by relying on reduced forces that show our capability—and readiness—to respond to whatever may arise. . . .

Role of Nuclear Forces in Europe

NATO [leaders] should also assess the future of US nuclear forces in Europe. As democracy blooms in Eastern Europe, as Soviet troops return home and tanks are dismantled, there is less need for nuclear systems of the shortest range. NATO [leaders] should accelerate ongoing work within the alliance to determine the minimum number and types of weapons that will be needed to deter war—credibly and effectively.

In light of these new political conditions and the limited range and flexibility of short-range nuclear missile forces based in Europe, I have reviewed our plan to produce and deploy newer, more modern, short-range nuclear missiles to replace the Lance system now in Europe. We have almost finished the research and development work for these new missiles. But I have decided, after consulting with our allies, to terminate the follow-on to [the] Lance program. I have also decided to cancel any further modernization of US nuclear artillery shells deployed in Europe.

There are still short-range US—and many more Soviet—nuclear missile systems deployed in Europe. We are prepared to negotiate the reduction of these forces as well, in a new set of arms control talks. I will urge my colleagues to agree on the broad objectives for these future US-Soviet negotiations and begin preparations within the alliance for these talks. . . .

In taking these steps, the United States is not going to allow Europe to become "safe for conventional war." There are few lessons so clear in history as this. Only the combination of conventional forces and nuclear forces have ensured peace in Europe.

But every aspect of America's engagement in Europe—military, political, and economic—must be complementary. And one place where they all come together is in the Conference on Security and Cooperation in Europe—an organization of 35 states of Europe and North America. The CSCE is already a beacon for human rights and individual freedoms. Now, it must take on a broader role.

Strengthening CSCE

So the fourth task for NATO [leaders] is to reach common allied objectives for the future of CSCE. It can help the victorious forces of democracy in Eastern Europe secure their revolutions, and—as they join the commonwealth of free nations—be assured a voice in the new Europe.

The CSCE should offer new guidelines for building free societies—including setting standards for truly free elections, adopting measures to strengthen the rule of law, and pointing the way in the needed, but painful, transition from centralized, command economies to free markets.

The CSCE can also provide a forum for political dialogue in a more united Europe. I agree with those who have called for regular consultations among senior representatives of the CSCE countries. We should consider whether new CSCE mechanisms can help mediate and settle disputes in Europe. . . .

Stability and Peace

In Eastern Europe, in this hemisphere, the triumph of democracy has cast its warm light on the face of the world like a miraculous dawn. But the outcome of this struggle for freedom is not ordained, and it will not be the work of miracles. . . .

I am convinced that our work to protect freedom—to build free societies—will safeguard our own peace and prosperity.

The security of Europe and the world has become very complex in this century. But America's commitment to stability and peace is profoundly clear. Its motivation derives from the strength of our forefathers—from the blood of those who have died for freedom—and for the sake of all who would live in peace.

Every voice, every heart's commitment to freedom, is important. There is a story about a man trying to convince his son that in the struggle for freedom, every voice counts. They stood in a valley, watching the snow fall on a distant mountain. "Tell me the weight of a snowflake," the man said.

"Almost nothing," answered the boy.

As the snow swirled around them, up on the mountain they saw an avalanche whose thunder shook the earth. "Do you know which snowflake caused that?" the old man asked.

"I don't," answered the boy.

"Maybe," said the man, "like the last snowflake that moves a mountain, in the struggle for freedom, a single voice makes a world of difference."

America's mission in Europe, like millions of individual decisions made for freedom, can make a world of difference.

"It is now time for [European nations] to reassume full responsibility for their own defense."

Europe No Longer Needs U.S. Protection

Rosemary Fiscarelli

The U.S. has stationed troops in Europe since the end of World War II to deter a Soviet attack. Now that the Cold War is over, Europe no longer needs to rely on the U.S. for protection, Rosemary Fiscarelli argues in the following viewpoint. Fiscarelli maintains that the Soviet Union is no longer a threat to Europe and that Europe can now afford to protect itself. Fiscarelli is a foreign policy analyst at the Cato Institute, a public policy think tank in Washington, D.C.

As you read, consider the following questions:

1. What does the author mean when she says that NATO's belief in "burden sharing" has now become "burden shedding"?
2. Why did many European nations cut their defense spending in 1989, according to Fiscarelli?
3. Why does the author believe that continued U.S. involvement in Europe will only cause tension between the allies?

Rosemary Fiscarelli, "NATO Confronts the 1990s." Reprinted from *USA Today* magazine, January 1991, © 1991 by the Society for the Advancement of Education.

Over the past several years, the specter of "burden sharing," which traditionally has haunted the North Atlantic Treaty Organization (NATO), has been transformed into "burden shedding." The traditional focus of intra-alliance disputes has been on who will bear what share of the financial, military, and other responsibilities. The new phenomenon of burden shedding consists of unilateral disarmament and defense budget cutting measures by various NATO members with a view to reaping a peace dividend in this new era of lowered tensions. Burden shedding is likely to be the divisive issue of the 1990s for NATO in the same way that burden sharing was in earlier times. That transformation, while significant, should not be allowed to obscure the fundamental and inherent imbalance in NATO's structure—namely, the U.S. guarantee of European geopolitical and military security.

When the North Atlantic Treaty was signed in 1949, the signatories envisioned a cooperative defense organization wherein each member-state would contribute equitably to the collective security. In the early days, many of the European nations, still recovering from the devastation of World War II, understandably were not in a position to contribute as much to the alliance as was the U.S. Gradually, however, many Americans began questioning why the European allies still were relying on the U.S. for their defense and not assuming more responsibility for NATO.

Failure of the Allies to Contribute

In response to economic concerns and a perception of increasing vulnerability to a rising Soviet threat, NATO adopted a policy in 1977 that formally required each member of the integrated military command to augment its contributions to the common defense by increasing its spending three percent per year after adjusting for inflation. That goal rarely has been met by any of the European allies, much less maintained on a consistent year-to-year basis. In contrast, during that same period, the U.S. engaged in an intensive military build-up aimed primarily at beefing up NATO defenses.

The three percent goal engendered rancorous burden sharing debates on both sides of the Atlantic over exactly what constituted a fair distribution of responsibilities. Some argued that defense expenditure, usually measured as a percentage of GNP [gross national product], was not by itself an accurate indicator of burden sharing. Consequently, elaborate schemes were developed to measure each ally's contribution in terms of such factors as numbers of active-duty, reinforcement, and reserve military personnel and amounts and types of equipment and weapons systems each member-state contributes. In turn, those quantifiable factors were measured against each member's population and its GNP. Finally, such less-quantifiable factors as the member-state's geographic proximity to the likely points of engagement were considered in determining its fair share of the burden.

© R. Lurie. Reprinted with permission.

Disputes over burden sharing raged throughout the 1980s. In particular, the demonstrations by masses of West Europeans in 1983 against the installation of intermediate-range nuclear missiles in Western Europe (in spite of the fact that they were the result of an alliance-wide determination of need) incited enormous resentment against the allies on the part of American taxpayers. As a result, the Department of Defense now is required statutorily to make an annual report on allied contributions to the common defense. In addition, the U.S. House of Representatives set up a special panel to study the issue. So persistent is concern over equity that our NATO delegation also includes an "ambassador for burden sharing." During most of the 1980s, the burden sharing debates, notwithstanding the Department of Defense's and the Eurogroup's efforts to the contrary, focused on the financial contributions of the allies.

With the arrival of Mikhail Gorbachev and his plans to reform the Soviet Union drastically, however, the Western allies, European and American alike, gradually began to believe that the Soviet threat, the glue that kept the alliance from unraveling, was declining. The watershed point in those events was Gorbachev's address to the United Nations in December, 1988, in which he pledged to withdraw unilaterally substantial numbers of Soviet forces from Eastern Europe. That move was a clear break with past initiatives in that it did not require reciprocal cuts from NATO, and it seemed to signal Soviet recognition that their security goals could be met with lower, less-threatening force levels.

Responses to Gorbachev's announcement varied. In the U.S., it was greeted with cautious optimism, but no substantive action. In Europe, however, a curious phenomenon emerged. Before a single Soviet soldier was withdrawn and—perhaps even more significant—before the conventional force reduction (CFE) talks began, European members of NATO began to make unilateral reductions of their own. In Belgium, the Parliament voted to cut military spending by nearly two percent, and it was announced that the Belgians would withdraw three air squadrons and an armored battalion from the NATO forces in West Germany. The Danes passed a three-year budget that featured zero growth of military expenditures, and the French Defense Ministry announced plans to reduce outlays.

That trend accelerated as 1989 progressed. In August, West German Defense Minister Gerhard Stoltenberg called for a study examining the feasibility of cutting the West German military, the Bundeswehr, by 22% (from 486,000 to 400,000). The Germans also announced a 57% drop (from 188 to 80) over the next 10 years in the number of their ships deployed on the North and Baltic seas. In September, the departing chief of staff of the Canadian Forces acknowledged that Canada seriously was considering withdrawing its forces from Europe. In October, NATO's Supreme Allied Commander, Europe, Gen. John Galvin, complained that the alliance had suffered approximately a 10% reduction in military capabilities because of those unilateral cuts.

Cuts Made Before Fall of Berlin Wall

It is perhaps easy in hindsight to think that all those moves were made in response to the easing of tensions following the collapse of Moscow's East European empire. It is important to note, however, that those moves largely were made *before* the

Berlin Wall was breached and *before* the Soviets renounced the Brezhnev Doctrine.

That timing is significant for two reasons. First, the obligation of all member-states of the alliance to defend against any aggressive moves that might have been made by the U.S.S.R., or the Warsaw Pact collectively, remained unchanged. If the Soviets had invaded Hungary, Poland, Czechoslovakia, and/or East Germany in an attempt to put down the anti-communist revolutions going on in those countries, such an attempt easily might have embroiled NATO as well. Under those circumstances, because of the cuts made by the allies, the U.S. unfairly would have had to shoulder an even greater portion of the burden. Second, the allies made their reductions unilaterally. In stark contrast with their persistent demands that the U.S. always diligently consult them and not indulge in "reckless Reykjavikism," they blithely made decisions affecting alliance commitments without any intra-alliance discussion.

The revolutions in Eastern Europe only have increased the hemorrhaging West European defense cuts. In January, 1990, the Belgian Defense Minister indicated that his country was considering withdrawing 25,000 of its troops (of a total of 28,000, or 89%) assigned to NATO duty in West Germany. Similarly, the Dutch have announced that one-fifth of their forces stationed in Germany will be withdrawn and that 11% of their NATO-dedicated F-16's will be eliminated. Even Washington's staunchest allies, the British, are undergoing a massive defense review and are contemplating large cuts. Those primarily would affect the British Army of the Rhine and the Royal Air Force personnel stationed in West Germany, which comprise a large portion of the British contribution to NATO.

In the course of all the reductions, there have been ongoing talks in Vienna about reducing both NATO and Warsaw Pact conventional forces in Europe, the CFE negotiations. In general, the CFE negotiators are striving to arrive first at a codifiable balance of NATO and Warsaw Pact conventional forces in Europe, and subsequently to reduce each alliance's forces to a lower level of balance. In fact, events have outstripped the pace of the negotiations and, in both pacts, member-states are making unilateral reductions willy-nilly. CFE, obviously, can not be relied upon to resolve the asymmetries in NATO burden sharing.

Washington's Uncertain Response

The American response to the allies' cuts has been to try to stem the flow by holding fast. The November, 1989, defense authorization bill called for maintaining the existing ratio of U.S. to total NATO forces in Europe. The logic behind that measure was that further unilateral reductions would be prevented if the allies did not feel that they had to beat the U.S. in the race to shed defense burdens. In point of fact, that tactic has failed, but even more significant is the absence of a justification for U.S. maintenance of the current level of support for European security. Given the reduced need, a far lower ratio certainly is in order.

In a belated recognition of reality, the U.S. finally dropped its demand for compliance with the three percent policy on May 17, 1990, and it was discarded formally at the meeting of the NATO defense ministers a week later. The diminution of the Soviet/Warsaw Pact threat to NATO was cited as the official reason for dropping the three percent goal.

That reasoning, however, raises a more fundamental issue. If the threat has diminished, the U.S. should be able to make substantial reductions in its own military forces, especially those earmarked for NATO. The European allies, however, adamantly are opposed to significant U.S. reductions.

Strong Incentives

NATO's European members have strong domestic incentives for avoiding an American withdrawal. In West Germany, for example, a study noted that "a complete American troop withdrawal could have disastrous economic consequences for the areas near the bases." Also, several European allies (e.g., Italy, Norway, Denmark, and West Germany) have been facing severe shortfalls in manpower to meet their alliance commitments. The possibility of painlessly meeting a reduced level by continuing their reliance on U.S. protection is, therefore, highly attractive to them, and it comes at a very convenient time. An obvious reason for their opposition, however, is simple economics—why pay for something oneself when another party, larger and wealthier, will do so? The allies stand to make substantial gains by reducing their defense expenditures and plowing those resources back into their economies.

Beyond those economic incentives for maintaining the American security commitment to Europe, there is also a military motivation. In the unlikely event of a renewed Soviet threat, it is much simpler for the allies to continue to rely on the U.S.-provided insurance policy than to develop their own security arrangement.

Nonetheless, the fundamental issue is not that the allies are scrambling to shed their financial and military contributions to the alliance. The shift from burden sharing to burden shedding is merely the metamorphosis of a symptom. The underlying problem is the American security guarantee to Europe.

Throughout NATO's history, considerable tension has existed between the U.S. and the European allies because of the American security guarantee. As in times past, the Europeans are not yet willing to assume full responsibility for their own defense, and the Americans are restless about paying for the security of prosperous and capable allies. With the demise of the Cold War, Americans eagerly are anticipating a long-awaited peace dividend. If, however, the U.S. maintains its commitment to European security while the allies continue to decrease their own military efforts, we will, in effect, be signing over our peace dividend check to them.

It is also important to recognize that a reduced level of threat means that the requirements for meeting the threat are reduced as well. Traditionally, one of the arguments in support of an American security guarantee for Western Europe was that only the U.S., as a superpower, was in a position to counter the threat posed to Europe by the U.S.S.R.'s massive military capabilities. Whatever the merits of that argument in the past, it is clear that the situation has changed drastically. The collapse of the Warsaw Pact means that the Soviets can not count on Pact forces to support any aggressive moves. It also means that they would have to cross an uncooperative and probably antagonistic Eastern Europe to mount a conventional attack on the West *and* do so with diminished conventional forces. Although the U.S.S.R. retains a formidable strategic arsenal, the European allies are not without resources to deal with that threat. (All of this, of course, begs the question of what possibly could motivate the Soviets to launch an attack against Western Europe, or what they would hope to gain by such an undertaking.) The allies clearly and adequately can meet the reduced military threat.

A Fundamental Revolution

Europe is undergoing a fundamental revolution in the politico-military, as well as the economic and cultural, spheres. The economic unification of the European Community (EC), scheduled to be in place by the end of 1992, has been expanded to include a basic political unification at the behest of the French and the West Germans. Although this process began before the end of the Cold War, it now is occurring simultaneously with the demise of the anomalous bipolar world that we have known for the past 40 years.

Western Europe has recovered from the ravages of World War II and is poised to take its place among the superpowers. The combined material and human resources of the EC surpass even those of the U.S. and the Japanese national economies. For many years, the allies have been developing various components of a defense organization, most notably the Western European Union (WEU). Their efforts, however, always have been eclipsed by NATO. It is now time for them to reassume full responsibility for their own defense. The U.S. should transfer full responsibility for European security to them. Clearly, choices about how their defenses are to be organized—whether under the auspices of the EC, the WEU, or another organization—must be made by the Europeans.

Nonetheless, only a transfer of responsibility from the U.S. to the Europeans will prevent the emergence of burden shedding disputes far more acrimonious than the traditional burden sharing controversies. Such disputes could cause NATO to break up in an atmosphere of mutual recrimination that would poison transatlantic relations for years. Even if that does not occur, the current trends hardly are favorable to American interests. As the Europeans pursue their unilateral burden shedding initiatives, the U.S. may be left with a greater *relative* NATO defense burden than it endured throughout the Cold War. If U.S. policymakers allow the Europeans to engage in preemptive reductions, while Washington "stands fast" as NATO's loyal guardian, there will be no peace dividend. If the American people are to reap the benefits they deserve from their investment, the U.S. must not perpetuate a security strategy designed for a Cold War world that has ceased to exist.

*"U.S. interests would be hurt if any power . . .
came to dominate certain regions of the Third
World."*

U.S. Involvement in the Third World Is Necessary

Mark N. Katz

During the Cold War, the U.S. and the Soviet Union used economic and military aid to expand their respective political ide-
ologies and power in the Third World. Now that the Cold War is
over, some experts contend that the U.S. has no reason to be involved in the Third World. In the following viewpoint, Mark N.
Katz disagrees with this position. Katz believes that political instability in the Third World will increase and leaders such as
Saddam Hussein will continue to attempt to gain regional control. The U.S. must maintain a military presence in the Third
World to preserve peace and protect U.S. interests, Katz concludes. The author is an assistant professor of government and
politics at George Mason University in Fairfax, Virginia.

As you read, consider the following questions:

1. How did the Reagan Doctrine affect the Third World, in the
   author's opinion?
2. Why does Katz believe China poses a threat to peace in the
   Third World?
3. What role can America's allies play in preserving peace in
   the Third World, in the author's opinion?

Reprinted from *The Washington Quarterly,* vol. 14, no. 1, "Beyond the Reagan Doctrine," by
Mark N. Katz, by permission of The MIT Press, Cambridge, MA and the Center for Strategic and International Studies. Copyright 1991 Massachusetts Institute of Technology and
the Center for Strategic and International Studies.

It has become commonplace by now to note that enormous changes have occurred in international relations, and that these changes will affect both the role of the United States in the world and U.S. foreign policy. But how exactly should U.S. foreign policy deal with lingering vestiges of the past and new problems of international security in an era of improved Soviet-U.S. relations? The answer is by no means clear because the full implications of the new international situation are not clear.

Response of the Bush Administration

In this uncertain environment, the Bush administration initially adopted the prudent course of pursuing those foreign policies that were successful in the past: supporting the North Atlantic Treaty Organization (NATO), continuing good relations with China, and opposing Marxist and other radical Third World regimes backed by Moscow, among others. This impulse was understandable. What worked in the past should not be lightly abandoned. Indeed, the pursuit of these policies played a large role in bringing about positive changes (from the Western point of view) in Soviet foreign and domestic policies. Why fix what isn't broken?

The Bush administration, however, has concluded that not all the policies of the past, however successful, should be carried into the future. This is particularly true of the Reagan Doctrine—the provision of military aid by the United States and its allies to guerrillas fighting against pro-Soviet Marxist Third World regimes. The Reagan Doctrine was undoubtedly instrumental in convincing President Mikhail S. Gorbachev that Moscow could not easily spread Marxist revolution to the Third World or keep Marxist regimes there in power cheaply. It is highly doubtful that the Soviets would have withdrawn their troops from Afghanistan or encouraged the Cubans and Vietnamese to withdraw theirs from Angola and Cambodia if the United States and its allies had not supported the guerrilla forces that the Marxists were trying to defeat.

In mid-1990, though, the Bush administration effectively began to turn away from the Reagan Doctrine in Cambodia and Afghanistan. For many years, Washington provided diplomatic and military backing to the Cambodian resistance coalition (the Marxist Khmer Rouge and two non-Communist movements) fighting against the Soviet- and Vietnamese-backed Hun Sen regime in Phnom Penh. Although the completion of the Vietnamese troop withdrawal from Cambodia in September 1989 did not induce the Bush administration to change this policy, in July 1990 Secretary of State James A. Baker III announced that the United States would no longer support the opposition coalition and would negotiate with Vietnam on a peace settlement for Cambodia.

Following the completion of the Soviet withdrawal from Afghanistan in February 1989, the Bush administration resisted Soviet calls for elections to be held there while the Marxist leader Najibullah remained in power. In mid-1990, however, Washington and Moscow reportedly made progress toward a peace settlement for Afghanistan in which both superpowers would cease arming their allies and elections would be held with the Najibullah regime still in power.

Third World Threats

Whether or not the United States faces a resurgence of the Soviet military threat, America will confront challenges to its global interests from terrorists, narcotics traffickers, Saddam Hussein-style dictators, and anti-American insurgency movements in the Third World. While none of these is as overwhelming as the Soviet threat, collectively they pose a steady, long-term challenge to such U.S. interests as the security of America's southern border, access to critical resources, preventing the spread of nuclear, biological, and chemical weapons, and encouraging the spread of democracy and free market institutions.

David A. Silverstein, The Heritage Foundation *Backgrounder,* March 12, 1991.

The Reagan Doctrine appears to remain fully operative only in Angola, although it would not be surprising if the United States and the Soviet Union soon agreed to an internal settlement there, especially as Cuban troops are withdrawn from Angola under the provisions of the December 1988 accords. . . .

Potential Regional Hegemony

The retreat of Soviet influence, however, does not mean that international relations will be marked by inevitable progress toward democracy, the peaceful resolution of all outstanding disputes under Soviet-U.S. direction, and increasing harmony among nations generally. Some serious threats to stability exist in regions of the developing world where certain states pursue hegemonic ambitions.

Even at the height of Soviet expansionism, the Soviet Union was by no means the only expansionist power in the Third World. While Moscow may have become disillusioned with expansionism, others have not. For while no one power poses the same threat of global expansionism as the Soviet Union once did, the behavior of several indicates that they are actively or potentially seeking hegemony within certain regions. And U.S. interests would be hurt if any power, not just the Soviet Union, came to dominate certain regions of the Third World such as the Persian Gulf, the Middle East, Southeast Asia, Latin America, or any of the world's important sea lanes.

The Persian Gulf. An Iranian victory in the Iran-Iraq war could have resulted in Iranian dominance over the entire Gulf region. The United States, eager to prevent Iran from gaining control over even more of the Gulf's oil reserves, worked to prevent this. The threat of Iranian hegemony over the region has subsided, but the threat of Iraqi hegemony arose when Saddam Hussein's forces overran Kuwait and menaced Saudi Arabia. The United States and its allies certainly have no interest in allowing Iraq to gain greater control over the Gulf, on which the West depends so heavily for its oil, or to obtain greater influence in the Middle East, which is already volatile enough. Iraq . . . and Iran . . . are thus greater threats than Moscow to U.S. interests in this vital region.

Southeast Asia. In Southeast Asia, U.S. and Western interests would suffer if any power were in a position to dominate the economically prosperous states of the Association of Southeast Asian Nations (ASEAN). During the 1970s and 1980s, the United States and ASEAN saw an aggressive Vietnam, backed by the Soviet Union, as posing the greatest threat to regional security. In consequence, both worked with China to thwart Soviet and Vietnamese efforts to dominate Cambodia. The U.S. motive was not the strategic importance of Cambodia, but fear of what the Soviet Union and Vietnam would do next in the region if they succeeded in dominating that country.

Questioning China's Motives

Now, however, Vietnam has withdrawn its troops from Cambodia and neither Hanoi nor Moscow appears interested in pursuing an expansionist policy in the region. Yet, despite this change, China continues to provide substantial quantities of arms to the genocidal Khmer Rouge. In addition to being concerned about how the Khmer Rouge would behave if they returned to power, the United States and its allies ought to be concerned about China's motives. Why is China not satisfied with the decline of Soviet and Vietnamese influence in Cambodia? Does China seek to dominate Cambodia? If it succeeds in doing so, how will it behave toward ASEAN? Unlike the government of the Soviet Union, the ruling party in China has become increasingly authoritarian. If ASEAN was worth protecting from Soviet influence, it is surely worth protecting from Chinese influence too. And although the threat of expanding Soviet and Vietnamese influence in the region may not have disappeared, it is receding while the threat of expanding Chinese influence is growing.

The Indian Ocean. The United States and its allies have a strong interest in maintaining maritime access to the Indian Ocean, if only to secure the flow of oil from the Gulf. For years the Soviet Union attempted to constrain that access through proposing various "zone of peace" formulas. Moscow never really expected the West to accept them, but apparently hoped that the states of the region would, thereby limiting Western naval access.

Ed Gamble. Reprinted with permission.

Although the Soviets did not succeed in rousing the region's enthusiasm for this goal, and their efforts in pursuing it have notably flagged, one important nation—India—enthusiastically advocated limiting the naval presence of outside parties in the Indian Ocean. New Delhi may well pursue this goal because, if it could be achieved, India would have the largest naval presence in the region. How would India behave if it achieved naval dominance in the Indian Ocean? Could the West depend on India to safeguard its access to Gulf oil? India's often belligerent attitude toward its weaker South Asian neighbors appears to indicate a desire to dominate where it can. If India achieved greater influence in South Asia, how would it behave in the broader Indian Ocean region? Although India can hardly be said to pose as serious a threat of regional expansionism as Iraq or

China, New Delhi's policies are definitely a potential problem. Washington should be no less concerned about India's efforts to limit or exclude Western access to the Indian Ocean than it was about Moscow's.

Latin America. The United States has a strong interest in preventing any hostile power from gaining predominant influence in Latin America. This concern, the basis of the Monroe Doctrine, long predates the Cold War. Under Gorbachev, Soviet support for revolution in Latin America has declined markedly. But Cuban support for revolutions against U.S.-supported governments continues, especially in Central America. What is Fidel Castro's goal in seeking to promote revolution? Does he aspire to some form of regional hegemony? Even if his actions are not supported by the Soviet Union, his efforts to extend his influence at the expense of the United States are clearly undesirable from Washington's point of view.

Hegemons and U.S. Foreign Policy

The United States has a strong interest in seeing that states aspiring to hegemony do not succeed. Hegemonic powers could cause serious problems for U.S. interests, and not just by constraining or excluding a regional U.S. presence. Even in regions that are remote or have little strategic value to the United States, a hegemon could threaten U.S. interests in other more important regions.

U.S. concern for the future of the Third World, then, is in one sense similar to its past concern: to prevent regional hegemony. The difference is that while the United States was primarily concerned about preventing Soviet efforts to achieve hegemony in various regions in the past, it should now be concerned to prevent any regional hegemony. . . .

Some of the same military policies Washington pursued in order to thwart Soviet hegemonism can also be employed to thwart regional hegemonies. These include providing security assistance for defensive purposes to countries being threatened, diplomatic efforts aimed at denying military aid to aggressive nations, supplying weapons to nations in conflict with hegemonic powers, or preventing hegemonic powers from interrupting the sea lines of communication on which the targets of their aggression depend (just as the United States and others protected Kuwaiti oil shipping against Iranian attack).

A serious problem is posed by the buildup of substantial military forces by aspiring hegemons with which vulnerable neighbors cannot cope militarily. The United States will face certain dilemmas in such cases. When and how should it become directly involved militarily to protect weaker nations against threatening states? It is far from certain that Americans would tolerate direct involvement in a protracted conflict to prevent regional hegemony if they did not perceive themselves as directly threatened or their allies as worth defending.

In the past, the United States has relied on the threat of nuclear attack to deal with a militarily robust opponent in Europe, but this strategy does not translate easily to the developing world. There are several reasons: the U.S. public would be unlikely to support such a policy; aspiring hegemons might not believe the United States would actually employ nuclear weapons, or they would pursue their aims in a more piecemeal way against which nuclear retaliation would be less appropriate or credible; and some potential hegemons already or may soon possess nuclear weapons and might be able to deter U.S. use of nuclear weapons because they could retaliate against U.S. interests, or the United States itself. . . .

The Difficulty of Defending Weaker States

Is this an exaggerated portrait of the real security dilemmas the United States faces in the Third World? Perhaps not. Kuwaiti armed forces were obviously unable to deter or prevent Iraq from conquering their country. The large number of troops that the United States and other countries sent to defend Saudi Arabia is indicative of the enormous effort needed to defend weaker states against regional aggressors.

Iraq is not the only example. If there is war between India and Pakistan, and if India emerges a militarized winner (and especially if the war has a nuclear component), who in the region will not fear the consequences? What if an expansionist Khmer Rouge regime is ensconced in Cambodia and backed by China, and turns its attention toward Thailand? What if several attempts to achieve regional hegemony occur simultaneously?

U.S. interests would be best served by the emergence of regional balances of power rather than acute threats to achieve hegemony because the requirements for maintaining stability will be far less than those of restoring stability once it has been upset by an ambitious and well-armed regional military power. The United States cannot achieve this goal alone. Cooperation with its Western allies on problems of regional security is growing more important, not less. Support for beleaguered Third World allies would be easier to muster, and the isolation of aspiring hegemons easier to achieve, if the United States, Europe, and Japan acted in concert than if the United States acted alone. Such cooperation would signal to those contemplating aggressive behavior that they could not play off the Western powers against each other—a danger that may grow when Western nations no longer fear a common Soviet threat. Maintaining regional balances of power would be more difficult if the Western allies disagreed over whether a particular nation was pursuing a hegemonic policy, or if some sold weapons to an aggressive state while others sought to deny them. Close collaboration among the Western allies will be necessary to ensure that such scenarios do not arise. . . .

The Threat of Expansionism

Instead of a new age of peace in the Third World, the post-Cold War era may well witness the pursuit of expansionist policies by several regional powers. As Iraqi aggression has shown, the hegemonic ambitions of even relatively small states can have extremely serious repercussions throughout the world as well as in a particular region. No one regional power's expansionism poses the same worldwide threat as Soviet expansionism did in the past. But because regional hegemonism does pose serious threats to U.S. security interests, and because there are numerous potential hegemons in the developing world, the task of deterring and countering regional expansionism will require a more flexible and sophisticated U.S. foreign policy in the post-Cold War era than did countering Soviet expansionism in the past.

"No national-security justification exists for U.S. commitment to Third World intervention."

U.S. Involvement in the Third World Is Unnecessary

Stephen Van Evera

Stephen Van Evera teaches political science at the Massachusetts Institute of Technology in Cambridge. In the following viewpoint, Van Evera asserts that U.S. involvement in the Third World neither protects U.S. interests nor promotes democracy in the region. Van Evera believes that the only role the U.S. has in the Third World is to protect human rights—something that he believes cannot be done through military intervention.

As you read, consider the following questions:

1. Why does Van Evera believe the Soviets are unable to build a Third World empire?
2. How does the author support his assertion that the Third World is unimportant?
3. What examples does Van Evera give to show that U.S. intervention does not promote democracy in the Third World?

Stephen Van Evera, "The Case Against Intervention," *The Atlantic,* July 1990. This article originally appeared in the March 1990 issue of *Defense and Disarmament Alternatives,* and is reprinted here with the author's permission.

In Europe the Cold War is over, but the Bush Administration is still waging it without letup in the Third World. . . .

In Cambodia the Administration supports a coalition dominated by the Khmer Rouge, which seeks to oust the Vietnam-installed Hun Sen government. In Angola it backs an extremely violent rebellion by the National Union for the Total Independence of Angola (UNITA). In Afghanistan it continues to sustain a rebellion by seven *mujahideen* groups against the Najibullah regime. In El Salvador it supports the right-wing ARENA [Nationalist Republican Alliance] government against the Marxist Farabundo Martí Front for National Liberation (FMLN). Discussions to end all four wars have begun, but so far the Bush Administration has adopted extreme negotiating positions, stalling progress toward peace. The Administration has also begun a new intervention, in Peru, and has supported lesser American involvement in civil conflicts in Guatemala and the Philippines.

The Administration should bring these proxy wars to a quick end. It should also drop the interventionist foreign policy they reflect. Third World intervention never made sense, even at the height of the Cold War. It makes less sense with that war's demise. Accordingly, the United States should cut its intervention forces and avoid further interventions except in a narrow range of circumstances.

Intervention for Security?

Throughout the Cold War, proponents of U.S. intervention made two principal claims: first, that Third World interventions protect U.S. national security by preserving the global balance of power, and second, that interventions promote democracy, thereby promoting human rights. Both arguments were false in the past, are false now, and would remain false even if the Soviet Union regained its strength and returned to pursuing an aggressive foreign policy.

The security argument for intervention incorporates several related assumptions:
- The Soviet Union desires an empire in the Third World.
- It aims to seize this empire by backing the expansion of subordinate Third World leftist states and movements.
- These leftists would make major gains unless the United States intervened.
- The Soviet Union would exploit those gains.
- Such gains would add significantly to Soviet military strength, ultimately tipping the world balance of power in the USSR's favor, thus threatening American national security.

This argument has underlain U.S. interventions in Iran, Guatemala, Indochina, Cuba, the Dominican Republic, Chile,

Grenada, Nicaragua, El Salvador, Angola, and elsewhere since 1945. It has three major defects. First, Soviet tolerance of the democratic upheavals in Eastern Europe signals the waning of Soviet expansionism worldwide, and perhaps its total abandonment. Eastern Europe matters far more to the USSR than any Third World region; Soviet leaders who concede their empire in Eastern Europe cannot still be dreaming of colonizing much less valuable Third World areas. Hence there is little Soviet imperial thrust left for U.S. interventions to blunt.

Second, even if it had the will, the Soviet Union lacks the capacity to colonize the Third World. Today it can barely control the empire within its borders, as unrest in the Baltic republics, Transcaucasia, and Central Asia reveals. Overseas colonialism is

---

End Proxy Wars

The cold war is over in Europe, but the United States is still waging the cold war without letup in the third world. A large chunk of the Bush administration's proposed FY [fiscal year] 1991 defense budget is allocated to forces optimized for third world intervention, including 15 aircraft carriers that have little function other than intervention, and 10 light army and marine divisions. Less expensive, but more important in human terms, the Bush administration continues to wage four gruesome proxy wars against leftist regimes and movements in the third world. . . .

The administration should bring these proxy wars to a quick end. It should also drop the interventionist foreign policy they reflect. Extensive third world intervention never made sense even at the height of the cold war, and makes even less sense with its demise. Accordingly, the United States should cut its intervention forces and avoid further interventions except in a narrow range of circumstances.

Defense and Disarmament Alternatives, March 1990.

---

unthinkable.

But even if the Soviets recovered their unity and their appetite for a Third World empire, they could not seize one. Soviet military forces are designed primarily for land war in Europe and for intercontinental nuclear war with the United States, not for Third World intervention. Nor can the Soviet Union gain an empire by promoting leftist revolution or expansion by Soviet proxy states, because the centrifugal force of nationalism tears the bonds between proxy and master. As a result, Third World leftists tend to be unruly proxies, seldom following Soviet dictates except when pushed into the Kremlin's arms by American bellicosity. This is underlined by the unfraternal relations among communist states, and illustrated by the conflicts that have often flared between the Khmer Rouge and Vietnam, Vietnam and China, China and the Soviet Union, the Soviet Union and Yugoslavia, and the Soviet Union and Albania.

In addition, the USSR is now evolving away from communism. This further discredits the notion that the Soviets can organize a transnational communist empire, since the leaders of the empire are themselves abandoning the ideology that would allegedly be able to glue it together.

The Unimportance of the Third World

Third, even large Soviet gains in the Third World would not tip the global balance of power, because by the best measure of strategic importance—industrial power—the Third World ranks very low. All of Latin America has an aggregate GNP [gross national product] less than half that of Japan. All of Africa has an aggregate GNP below that of Italy or Great Britain. The aggregate GNP of the entire Third World is below that of Western Europe. Modern military power is distilled from industrial power; thus the Third World has little military potential and correspondingly little strategic significance.

Moreover, the nuclear revolution has reduced the Third World's strategic importance to a level far below even the modest one that its industrial strength might indicate. Nuclear weapons represent a defensive revolution in warfare. They make conquest among great powers almost impossible, because a victor must now destroy nearly all of an opponent's nuclear arsenal—an insuperable task. As a result, the nuclear revolution has devalued the strategic importance of all conquered territory, including Third World territory, because even huge conquests would not provide the conqueror with enough technical or material assets to give it decisive nuclear superiority over another great power. Hence industrial regions that mattered greatly before the nuclear age now matter only somewhat, while Third World regions that formerly mattered little now matter even less. Some interventionists assert that the Third World has strategic importance because of the alleged Western dependence on Third World raw materials or the alleged strategic value of military bases in Third World areas. Both claims are much overdrawn. Oil is the only Third World material on which the West depends to any degree. The West imports many other materials from the Third World, but at modest additional cost all of them could be produced locally in the West or otherwise replaced. Bases, too, could be replaced by longer-range forces, or moved to new locations if a given country denied basing rights to the United States.

If any of these three criticisms is accepted, the security case for intervention fails. It requires that the Soviets seek a Third World empire, that they be able to gain one, and that the empire add decisively to their power; otherwise the world balance of power is not threatened, leaving no problem for intervention to solve. The absence of all three conditions creates a very strong case against intervention. Moreover, two of these three conditions were absent before the Gorbachev revolution, and would remain absent even if that revolution were reversed.

In short, no national-security justification exists for U.S. commitment to Third World intervention.

Democracy by Bayonet?

During the 1980s proponents of intervention supplemented security arguments with claims that American interventions promote democracy. This argument fails on both logical and historical grounds.

Democracy requires suitable social and economic preconditions: a fairly equal distribution of land, wealth, and income; high levels of literacy and economic development; cultural norms conducive to democracy, such as traditions of tolerance, free speech, and due process of law; and few deep ethnic divisions. Most of the Third World lacks democracy because these preconditions are missing. Moreover, it would require vast social engineering, involving long and costly post-intervention occupations, to introduce them. American taxpayers clearly would

---

The Scars from Intervention

After forty years of Cold War intervention in Latin America, Asia, Africa, and Europe, the notion of the United States continuing to control events in the third world to preserve a way of life congenial to U.S. policy has become unrealistic. There are scars on the body politic. Public opinion polls have consistently shown that a considerable sector believes "covert actions" are unproductive, partly as a result of the ongoing series of scandals that follow from them. The tactics, the policies, indeed the very strategy of the Cold War have become unsuitable.

Saul Landau, *Winning America: Ideas and Leadership for the 1990s,* 1988.

---

not support extravagant projects of this sort.

In the past, U.S. interventions have generally failed to bolster democracy. They have left dictatorship more often than democracy in their wake; Washington has often subverted elected governments that opposed its policies; and many U.S.-supported "democratic" governments and movements were not at all democratic. Overall, this record suggests that the United States lacks both the will and the ability to foster democracy. . . .

The undemocratic nature of American policies results partly from a pronounced bias in favor of elites. The Carter Administration's support for the Nicaraguan oligarchy was not unique; elsewhere in the Third World, American policy has bolstered the power of local anti-democratic elements, who have then blocked the social leveling that democratization requires. In South Korea, U.S. policy favored the rightist elite from the early days of the postwar occupation. In the Philippines the United States aligned itself with the upper-class *ilustrado* elite after seizing the islands in 1898-1899, and again when it recovered the Philippines from Japan in 1944-1945. In Guatemala the CIA-sponsored Castillo Armas government (1954-1957) repealed universal suffrage and dispossessed peasant beneficiaries of earlier land reforms, leaving Guatemala among the most stratified societies in the world. Throughout Latin America the Alliance for Progress, founded partly to promote social equality, was co-opted by oligarchic governments that ran it for the benefit of wealthy elites. As a result, the alliance in fact increased social stratification.

America's ambivalence toward Third World democracy is more starkly manifest in its recurrent subversion of elected Third World governments that have pursued policies distasteful to the United States. There have been eleven prominent instances since 1945 in which elected nationalist or leftist regimes in the Third World have adopted policies that disturbed Washington. In nine of these cases—Iran (1953), Guatemala (1954), British Guiana (1953-1964), Indonesia (1957), Ecuador (1960-1963), Brazil (1961-1964), the Dominican Republic (1965), Costa Rica (the mid-1950s), and Chile (1970-1973)—the United States attempted to overthrow the elected government (or, in the Dominican case, to prevent its return to power) and most of the time succeeded. In the other two cases—Greece (1967) and Jamaica (1976-1980)—evidence of American subversion is less clear-cut but is nevertheless substantial.

In short, American leaders have favored democracy only when it has produced governments that support American policy. Otherwise they have sought to subvert democracy.

The thuggish character of America's Third World proxies also reveals American ambivalence toward Third World democracy. America's client regimes in Central America are illustrative. The U.S.-backed governments of El Salvador, Guatemala, and Honduras hold regular elections, but none passes the first test of democracy: that those elected control government policy. Instead, the army and the police effectively rule all three countries; the civilian governments are hood ornaments on military vehicles of state. If civilian officials defied the military, they would promptly be removed by assassination or coup. Knowing this, they do the military's bidding. Moreover, the preconditions for fair elections—free speech, a free press, and the freedom to vote, organize, and run for office—cannot develop because of government death squads that systematically murder critics of the government. The official terror has reached vast proportions in El Salvador, where the government has murdered more than 38,000 people since 1979, and in Guatemala, where the government has murdered 140,000 since 1970. "Fair" elections are impossible amid such slaughter.

In sum, the United States lacks the means to institute democracy by intervention, and apparently lacks the will. There is little reason to expect more-democratic results from future interventions. Accordingly, the advancement of democracy is an unpersuasive reason for intervention. . . .

The United States should stop intervening "to protect national security" or "to strengthen Third World democracy," since the results of intervention seldom serve either purpose. And the United States should never use force on a large scale in the Third World, because no U.S. interest in the Third World can justify paying large costs or taking large numbers of lives. Protecting human rights is America's main interest in the Third World—but human rights are seldom served by large-scale violence.

Formulating a Defense Strategy

When a military conflict occurs in a foreign nation, the U.S. president and the Congress must decide how to respond. They may decide to send troops, military support, or aid. Many factors contribute to this decision. For example, if the conflict threatens U.S. national security, affects U.S. economic interests, or involves the abuse of human rights, the U.S. may become involved militarily.

The following activity describes a moment in history when the United States had to decide whether or not to use the military to solve a regional conflict in another part of the world. Analyzing this international crisis will help you determine what role you think the U.S. should play in world defense.

Read the following scenario, which describes an international crisis that took place in 1950. Then try to determine the most appropriate U.S. response to the crisis.

The Korean Conflict

Korea is a peninsular Asian nation that borders China on the north and the Sea of Japan on the south. Between 1910 and 1945, Korea was part of the Japanese empire. At the end of World War II, Allied leaders determined that Korea should be given its independence. Just as Germany was divided between the Soviet Union and Western nations, so was Korea divided, with the U.S. occupying the nation south of the 38th parallel and the Soviets occupying the region north of this line.

The Soviets quickly installed a communist government headed by dictator Kim Il-Sung. The U.S. organized a government headed by anticommunist Syngman Rhee. It soon became obvious that Korea had become two separate nations, and hopes of reuniting them became dimmer as time passed. In 1948, South Koreans officially elected Syngman Rhee president and established the nation as the Republic of Korea. That same year, the communist government in the north appointed Kim Il-Sung premier and designated the nation as the Democratic People's Republic of Korea. Both nations, however, claimed rights to all of Korea. In 1949, the U.S. withdrew all of its occupying combat troops from South Korea.

61

However, the U.S. still doubted the stability of South Korea, and feared that North Korean and Chinese communists would take over South Korea. The South Korean government shared this fear, and asked for U.S. military aid. The U.S. provided South Korea with economic aid, military advisors, and weapons. Even with this assistance, many U.S. officials were still concerned about the weakness of the south. Their concerns were vindicated on June 25, 1950, when North Korea invaded South Korea.

Part I

The U.S. has several options. It can:

a) send U.S. troops immediately to help the South Koreans repel the invasion

b) bring the issue before the United Nations and ask them to manage either a peaceful solution or organize an international military force to compel the North Koreans to withdraw

c) take no action and let North and South Korea settle the conflict between themselves

If you were the president of the United States, which of the above three options would you choose? Explain your reasoning.

Part II

Read the following facts concerning how the U.S. actually responded and how this response affected the Koreas and the U.S.

The U.S. response:

Two days after the invasion, the U.S. asked the United Nations Security Council to urge member nations to help South Korea repel the invasion. The resolution passed, since the Soviet Union, which would most likely have voted against the resolution, was at the time boycotting the UN. U.S. president Harry Truman ordered American air and naval forces to provide combat support to South Korea. He then committed U.S. ground forces to a multinational UN force headed by U.S. general Douglas MacArthur.

The outcome of U.S. actions: .

The war continued until 1953. At the request of the UN, twenty other nations assisted the U.S. and South Korea in the war. In November 1950, MacArthur's forces reached the Yalu River, which separates North Korea from Manchuria, a Chinese province. The Chinese crossed the Yalu and attacked UN forces, forcing them to retreat. Wishing to avoid a large-scale war, the UN refrained from attacking China and confined the war to Korea. By January 1951 the Chinese and North Koreans had pushed UN forces back into South Korea, south of Seoul. In March, UN forces liberated Seoul. In June, the two sides began negotiations, which lasted two years and resulted in the establishment of the 38th parallel as the boundary between North and South Korea. This, of course, was the boundary prior to the war. More than one million people were killed in the war, including 54,246 Americans. North Korea remained a communist nation under the authority of Kim Il-Sung, while South Korea continued to be a republic. To this day, the two nations are divided at the 38th parallel.

1. Did your decision differ from Truman's?

2. Do you think Truman made the right decision? Why or why not?

3. Does knowing Truman's decision and the outcome change your opinion concerning what the U.S. should have done? If so, how?

4. In general, what factors do you think the U.S. should consider before it commits American troops to a foreign conflict?

Periodical Bibliography

The following articles have been selected to supplement the diverse views presented in this chapter.

A.J. Bacevich
"New Rules: Modern War and Military Professionalism," *Parameters*, December 1990. Available from the Superintendent of Documents, Government Printing Office, Washington, DC 20402.

Richard Barnet
"An Illusion," *Harper's Magazine*, May 1991.

Marshall Brement
"Reaching Out to Moscow," *Foreign Policy*, Autumn 1990.

Stephen Budiansky
"Lessons from Desert Shield," *U.S. News & World Report*, September 10, 1990.

Ted Galen Carpenter
"An Independent Course," *The National Interest*, Fall 1990. Available from 1112 16th St. NW, Washington, DC 20036.

Eliot A. Cohen
"The Future of Force and American Strategy," *The National Interest*, Fall 1990.

Aaron L. Friedberg
"Is the United States Capable of Acting Strategically?" *Washington Quarterly*, Winter 1991. Available from MIT Press Journals, 55 Hayward St., Cambridge, MA 02142.

Raymond L. Garthoff
"Changing Realities, Changing Perceptions," *The Brookings Review*, Fall 1990. Available from The Brookings Institution, 1775 Massachusetts Ave. NW, Washington, DC 20036.

Nathan Glazer
"A Time for Modesty," *The National Interest*, Fall 1990.

Philip Gold
"Proof Is in Pudding for Deployment," *Insight*, September 24, 1990. Available from PO Box 91022, Washington, DC 20090-1022.

Andrew C. Goldberg
"Challenges to the Post-Cold War Balance of Power," *Washington Quarterly*, Winter 1991.

Michael T. Klare
"Policing the Gulf—and the World," *The Nation*, October 15, 1990.

Charles Krauthammer
"Must America Slay All the Dragons?" *Time*, March 4, 1991.

Michael Ledeen
"We *Are* Number One," *The American Spectator*, March 1991.

Should Women Serve in the U.S. Military?

AMERICA'S DEFENSE

Chapter Preface

American women have always played a supportive and some-times participatory role in America's wars. For many years, women's military organizations, such as the Women's Army Corps, were separate from the regular military. In the mid-1970s, women were officially integrated into the military and women's military organizations were discontinued. Today, men and women soldiers train and work side by side in noncombat jobs. Women make up 11 percent of the U.S. military. As increasing numbers of women enlist, there is still much debate concerning what positions women should hold—specifically, whether women should be al-lowed to participate in combat.

Many Americans view the issue as one of job equality: If women have the right to hold any job in society, they also have the right to hold any job in the military, including combat posi-tions. Americans such as psychologist Ruth Westheimer believe women's rights must extend to military duties. "All that is keeping women out of combat is the same discrimination we've faced breaking into every other male-dominated position," Westheimer states. She and others believe that women's physical, emotional, and mental abilities make them as capable soldiers as men.

But not all Americans see the issue as one of equal rights. To many, the battlefield is a unique workplace where women do not belong. Americans such as conservative columnist Suzanne Fields believe that because women are physically weaker than men, women cannot be effective soldiers and should not be in combat. As Fields states, "Readiness, efficiency, preparedness are the es-sential ingredients for a trained army, and most women—nearly all women—at their very best fall far short of fighting standards." In addition, Fields and others are concerned that the presence of women in combat will distract men from their duties, resulting in a less effective military.

Throughout the centuries, societies have debated the proper roles of men and women. The following chapter presents argu-ments concerning the modern controversy of what role women should play in the U.S. military.

"The policy of combat exclusion for women is impractical and inequitable."

Women Should Serve in Combat

Francine D'Amico

While women have been integrated into the U.S. military since the mid-1970s, they are still prohibited from serving in combat. In the following viewpoint, Francine D'Amico argues that excluding women from combat is illogical, inefficient, and unfair. D'Amico maintains that, as a result of changes in warfare, women are already serving in combat positions. She refutes the claims that women are too weak physically and psychologically to fight in battle. D'Amico is an assistant professor of politics at Ithaca College in New York.

As you read, consider the following questions:

1. Why do some men oppose the idea of women learning self-defense, in D'Amico's opinion?
2. What argument does the author give to the claim that pregnancy and family responsibilities will impede the effectiveness of women soldiers?
3. How has the nuclear age changed women's role in warfare, according to the author?

Francine D'Amico, "Women at Arms: The Combat Controversy," *Minerva Quarterly Report*, Summer 1990. Reprinted by permission of the Minerva Center, Arlington, Virginia.

By law and by policy, women in the United States' armed forces are excluded from combat. Yet the extent of women's integration into the military makes the exclusion untenable, as recent operations in Central America, the Persian Gulf, and northern Africa have illustrated. Women now constitute nearly eleven percent of US armed forces' personnel. They predominate in clerical/administrative, communications, and medical specialties, and serve in capacities vital to all branches of the defense establishment. In this sense, women are no longer "auxiliaries," i.e., temporary, nonessential helpers; their presence and skills are integral to the proper functioning of our modern military. Women are, as Michel Louis Martin has said with regard to the French military, a "critical mass" in today's armed forces. . . .

The term "combat" conjures a vivid mental image of uniformed soldiers trapped in a muddy foxhole, with a barrage of artillery raining all around. But this image captures only one frame in the shifting reality of military engagement, and is more a reminiscence of WWII [World War II] than a realistic description of contemporary combat. In modern warfare, combat ranges from terrorist attack to guerrilla ambush to the push-button variety, both telescoping and enlarging the distance between "combatants" and battlefield. The traditional "combat" v. "support" demarcation blurs as troop mobility and the range of conventional and nuclear weaponry expand. . . .

Objections to allowing women in combat may be categorized as physiological, psychological, military-strategic, and sociological-political.

Physiological Arguments

Many who defend the combat exclusion policy, such as George Gilder, argue that women's smaller stature and lack of "upper body strength" make them less useful combat soldiers than men. This argument has been challenged by Judith Hicks Stiehm, who points out that smaller stature didn't seem to hurt the Vietnamese. In fact, women may have a physical advantage in some types of warfare, such as guerrilla conflict, where their generally smaller size will make them smaller targets and their greater capacity to endure extremes of temperature and physical pain (witness childbirth) will help them survive. Of course, not all women are weaker/smaller than all men; one could compare the physical condition of an average 18-21 year old woman with that of a 48-51 year old man, or consider the disparity between a petite female athlete and an obese male non-athlete. Physical conditioning may be as great a determinant of strength as sex *per se*. Strength may bear little relation to stature, and its relation to military performance may be mitigated to some extent by technology, as sophisticated weaponry increases the distance between the soldier and the enemy forces.

Those opposed to sending women into combat cite women's presumed greater vulnerability to rape and sexual assault as a form of enemy torture if captured as sufficient reason to exclude them. In civilian society, a woman is raped *every six minutes*. Approximately half of all sexual assaults occur in the woman's own home, and many are perpetrated by men whom the women know (incest; marital and acquaintance rape). Many women suffer physical abuse/battery from their spouses or male companions. Keeping women at home doesn't keep them safe. This argument also reflects US isolation from recent conflicts; occupying forces frequently rape/abuse civilian women.

Mike Keefe. Reprinted with permission.

However, the rigorous physical conditioning and training in self-defense which they would receive as part of their military experience may go a long way toward helping them learn to protect themselves, as Judith Hicks Stiehm notes:

> When women are defenders and no longer confined to the category of the protected they are able to shake off the disabilities which attend dependency: low esteem, low level of information, and little sense of responsibility.

In fact, the idea that women may become their own protectors may be a large part of the reason that the idea of training women to fight (read "fight back") is so unpalatable to some men, as Gloria Steinem has argued. If women learn how to avoid becoming victims, what will happen to men's power over them in our society?

Psychological Arguments

While arguments about the psychology of warfare are closely linked to more routinely "military" considerations of the combat status of women such as deployment, psychology has been treated as a separate analytic category here for purposes of clarity. Those who support the combat exclusion policy argue that unit cohesiveness, based on what Lionel Tiger has called "male bonding," would be threatened by women's presence in combat units. George Gilder asserts that men's "natural aggressiveness" is necessary to success in battle but would be subject to the "softening" influence of women soldiers, thus endangering the mission and national security. Dorothy and Carl J. Schneider argue that combat exemption itself undermines morale, because of male personnel's resentment of the special treatment accorded to female personnel. As for the argument that the presence of women will inhibit men's "natural" aggressiveness, perhaps some mitigation is in order, given past incidents of excessive violence and abuse of power, as at My Lai.

Some analysts have conjectured that if women adopt the heretofore masculine activity of combat, men may abandon the warrior role altogether in search of some concrete confirmation of their masculinity (non-womanness):

> The trenches, combat service in the air, transport jobs in advanced positions, and even other . . . arenas of activity in the theater of war, are the last remaining stronghold of men. I suspect that men might rather vacate the arena altogether than share it with women.

In terms of US vulnerability to enemy attack, the prospect seems far from comforting. But in terms of progress toward the goal of world peace, men's abandonment of the international combat arena to women might be cause for celebration, given men's "track record" and women's allegedly greater tendency toward pacifism. . . .

Military-Strategic Arguments

Analysts concerned over the growing presence of women in the US armed forces argue that reliance on women impairs "readiness" and the ability for "rapid deployment," but this appears a *result* of the combat exclusion policy itself; if women were no longer excluded from combat, the services would have full flexibility for their posting, thus enhancing efficiency. For example, in 1985, 256 of the Air Force's 21,115 pilots were women, and 11.6% of the Air Force Academy cadet corps were women, yet these pilots and officers may not serve on fighter and bomber aircraft if the need arises due to combat engagement/casualty losses.

Some critics argue that servicewomen's pregnancy rate and family responsibilities impede deployment and cause logistical problems, but studies of women's v. men's service records indicate that women lose less time from their jobs for reasons of illness/disability than do men, and Mady Wechsler Segal notes that men as well as women have family responsibilities.

Some focus on the impact that women combatants' presence would have on battlefield behavior both within the US ranks and of corps by enemy. Linda Ewing worries that women's presence in combat units may cause "disproportionate losses" because US servicemen will take unnecessary risks to protect female combatants whom they perceive as vulnerable and because the enemy forces may fight with greater vigor to avoid the shame of defeat by/surrender to women. Phil Stevens argues that if the exclusion policy is abandoned, women's loss of noncombatant status will make them subject to greater "dehumanization" at the hands of their captors than has been experienced by previous women prisoners, and he suggests that policymakers' knowledge that women are held prisoner (and subsequent public outrage?) may "compromise hardline negotiations" in a conflict.

Both these lines of argument suggest that the problem is not with women in combat but with men's attitudes toward women in combat. Ewing's objections may be obviated by the routinization of women's presence in combat units, as Judith Hicks Stiehm has argued. Stevens' argument with regard to negotiation and compromise, if accurate, may be heralded as one way to mitigate the destructiveness of war. . . .

Sociological-Political Arguments

The "protective" principle, that is, the notion that women can and should be protected from the horrors of war, appears to underlie most objections to an elimination of the formal policy of combat exclusion. Why is this principle so strongly held, and how realisitic is reliance on this principle, given the scope of modern warfare? Anthropologist Margaret Mead suggested that the practice of arming men and not women may have to do with a "cultural imperative"—to allow for the reproduction of society. The lesson women are supposed to learn from the extinction of the Amazons, if such a culture has existed anywhere but in myth, is that arming women destroys the race—and, further, that challenging the sexual division of labor in any social context may upset the social equilibrium in the same manner, chiefly because of the disruption of reproduction and child-rearing. If women abandon their allotted tasks as wives/mothers, who can replace them? While men may learn to nurture children, they are ill-equipped to bear or breast-feed infants. Perhaps technological advances will someday open this possibility, but for now, women's monopoly on reproduction remains complete.

An analogy from the animal world is frequently used to argue that woman is unsuited for offensive warfare and may be unable to temper her brutality: the female animal will fight to the death in defense of her young. Mead argued that the near-universal reluctance to arm women was related to this observation:

> It is possible that the historic refusal to give women weapons, except very briefly and under exceptional circumstances, may be due not to a rejection of putting the power of death into the hands of those who give life, but rather because women who kill on behalf of the lives of their children are more implacable and less subject to chivalrous rules with which men seem to mute the savagery of warfare. It may be that women would kill too thoroughly and endanger the negotiations and posturings of armies, through truces and prisoner taking, with which nations . . . eventually manage uneasy breathing spaces between wars.

Mead surmised that the prohibition against arming women arose from a sexual division of labor in warfare: men fought offensively, "going off to war," while women fought defensively, protecting their homes and children from attack by invaders. Men became warriors in primitive society because of their relatively greater strength and mobility; women became defenders because of the more sedentary nature of their reproductive role.

Arming the Oppressed

Mead believed that men learn to observe set "rules of the game" in their pursuance of offensive warfare; they fight to establish order or for other limited objectives, whereas women fight to the death because they struggle for survival. Perhaps women, too, could learn the "rules of the game" in warfare and be taught to temper their ferocity. But I would offer a different interpretation of this pervasive practice: the reluctance to arm women may, instead, stem from a fear of putting weapons into the hands of the traditionally oppressed, of giving victims power over their abusers—cf. historical prohibitions against arming serfs, peasants, slaves, or men of the lower classes in earlier periods.

All societies hesitate to arm the "underclass" or exploited, witness the experience of Black males in the US armed forces.

During the Civil War, the Union Army admitted Black men, but only in racially segregated units where they were armed not

72

with guns but with picks and shovels, put to work building railroads, hauling supplies, and performing other manual labor. Military units remained racially segregated throughout WWI and WWII, and, once again, officials hesitated to arm Black men. Most were assigned to Supply Corps, Transportation, or other noncombatant positions. With racial integration of US armed forces during the Korean conflict, commanders continued to prefer posting Black servicemen to noncombatant jobs. During US involvement in Vietnam, top brass worried about the high proportion of Black vis-a-vis White inductees; their concern grew as the move toward the All Volunteer Force and demographic trends appeared to indicate that the enlisted ranks would be filled mainly by Black and Hispanic males. Their fear of arming Black men, especially during a time of Black political activism, encouraged military officials to actively recruit more qualified (read "white, educated") men—and even women, to fill certain jobs deemed suitably "feminine." Perhaps the notion of arming women—victims of male crimes of rape, sexual assault, and physical abuse—holds an even greater terror.

Why Women Should Fight

The National Organization for Women (NOW) has long believed that combat roles should be open to women for several reasons:

1. The prohibition of women from combat positions means that qualified women are denied promotions to better-paying jobs in the armed forces. . . .

2. Modern warfare is very different from World War I and II. Missiles and aircraft are now of tremendous importance, and women are trained and excel in the expertise needed to operate these systems.

3. Front lines are not the only place wars are fought. The greatest number of casualties of World War II were civilians bombed day after day in the cities of Europe and Japan.

4. Assigning military women to the rear support troops is no longer safe because modern military strategy aims to destroy support troops before assaulting those up front.

5. Women should have equal treatment with men. Gender should not exclude any person from rising to the top in any of the services.

Molly Yard, *American Legion Magazine*, May 1990.

There have, however, been many women who have crossed the line between defensive and offensive warfare; these warrior women have been mythologized, rendered either sub- or superhuman, e.g., the Amazon "She-Beasts" or the divine Joan of Arc. Women who have disregarded the allegedly "natural" sexual division of labor in warfare have been either desexed (saints) or hypersexed (exotic, man-killing nymphomaniacs). Female warriors are non-women, unnatural women, because they don't do those things which women are supposed to do: care for men and children, submit to male authority, and seek male "protection" (from other men!). The myths serve, then, to keep women in their "place": vulnerable to men.

Changes in the Nuclear Age

The nuclear age has changed the scope of war and has exploded the logic of this "protective principle." There can be no homefront v. battlefield dichotomy in a nuclear exchange; fallout from attacks on "military" targets will be an indiscriminant killer of soldiers and civilians alike. The reality of the nuclear era exposes the fallacy of the idea that we will have a choice about whether or not women "go to war"; the next war may come to us. There can be no homefront v. battlefield dichotomy in a nuclear exchange; fallout from "counter-force" attacks on military targets will be an indiscriminant killer of soldiers and civilians alike, and civilian populations are deliberately targeted in "counter-value" deterrence strategy. . . .

Women's Wishes

Do women want to be combatants? The question, unfortunately, seems to be considered irrelevant by policy-makers; they argue that the decision to arm women and to maintain or eliminate the policy of combat exclusion must be based on perceived military necessity rather than on considerations of women's wants or notions of equity. To some military planners, women are just one more resource in their arsenal; many manipulate egalitarian arguments about certain aspects of military service not to improve the life-chances of women but to serve the needs of the ephemeral "national security." Yet women's actual record of sacrifice as combatants, in counterpoint to their noncombatant status, demonstrates that equity must also be considered in the design of personnel policy. At present, women share the risk but not the recognition of combat service and continue to have little input into the military's decision-making process. Attention to this issue now is essential to future determinations regarding women's military "utilization." I concur with Representative Patricia Schroeder's assessment: the policy of combat exclusion for women is impractical and inequitable.

"We know that, by most measures, women are a bad buy for the military."

Women Should Not Serve in Combat

Brian Mitchell

Brian Mitchell, a former army infantry and intelligence officer, is the author of the controversial book *Weak Link: The Feminization of the American Military*, which criticizes women's ability to serve effectively in the military. In the following viewpoint, excerpted from his book, Mitchell asserts that women are physically and psychologically weaker than men and therefore make poor soldiers. The author concludes that allowing women to serve in combat will threaten the safety of the United States.

As you read, consider the following questions:

1. Why is the Department of Defense hesitant to repeal the combat exclusion laws, in the author's opinion?
2. What evidence does Mitchell give to support his belief that women are too weak to fight in combat?
3. Why does Mitchell believe that allowing women into the military has threatened the military's values?

There can be no doubt that the American military has undergone radical change since 1970. At that time, the role of women in the military was still following a long downward trend. After a failed attempt to involve large numbers of women in the military during the Korean War, military planners were convinced that American women would not play a significant role in any peacetime force. The number of women in service and the number of jobs open to them shrank steadily for fifteen years following the war. In 1967, the participation of women in the American military reached its lowest point since World War II, with barely 20,000 women in service, not including nurses. Women made up less than 2 percent of the total force.

Then the trend was abruptly reversed. The shift to the All-Volunteer Force and the political success of the American feminist movement combined to bring about a re-direction of military manpower thinking and a rapid expansion of the military use of women. In a very short time, the number of women increased fivefold. Today, the American military has more than 221,000 women in active service—10.3 percent of its total force. Fifteen percent of first-year students at the nation's service academies are female, and one out of every seven enlisted recruits is a woman. Only a handful of specialties and assignments are still closed to women, and each year sees more and more positions opened, thanks to the elastic quality of the so-called combat exclusion laws, which always seem to permit today what they were understood to forbid yesterday.

A Military Dependent upon Women

No other military in the world depends so heavily upon women. The U.S. employs more women as a percentage of its total force than any country on earth. Canada is second, with women representing 9.2 percent of its total force, followed by the United Kingdom with 5.1 percent. The Soviet Union's 4.4 million-member armed force includes only 10,000 women, performing largely clerical and medical work. Israel drafts women, but the jobs open to them are more limited than the jobs open to American military women during World War II. A handful of small, secure NATO [North Atlantic Treaty Organization] nations have opened combat units to women, but the numbers of women involved are very small, and expectations that they will ever actually see combat are even smaller.

The official position of the U.S. Department of Defense is that integration has proceeded without the slightest decline in the combat capabilities of the armed forces. The modern All-Volunteer Force is far superior to any earlier force of volunteers or conscripts, say defense officials. Today's recruits are the finest the services have ever seen: the best educated, the best motivated, the best behaved. As for women, official phraseology makes them "an integral part" of the armed forces. "We can't go to war without them," say the admirals and the generals; women are "here to stay." They perform "as well as or better than" the men. They are promoted faster. They add an air of civility to military service. Their effect on morale and readiness is positive.

For all the flattery that military women receive, one might expect the Defense Department to be eager to repeal the combat exclusions. After all, the department's official position is that the exclusion of women from combat is based solely on the cultural preference of the American people and not on any military consideration. Because repeal would expand greatly the pool of possible recruits and simplify the services' personnel management systems, enabling them to make more efficient use of all personnel, the only responsible action on the Pentagon's part should be to request that the laws be repealed.

A Matter of Biology

Women, of course, have no business in combat. It is not a matter of courage or intelligence. It is simple biology.

We have recorded history going back about 8,000 years and nowhere in it are there any instances where women successfully competed with men on the battlefield. Only the modern urban neurotic would discount 8,000 years of human experience as male prejudice.

Charley Reese, *Conservative Chronicle*, January 31, 1990.

A recent report on the All-Volunteer Force by the General Accounting Office, however, provides a clue as to why neither the Defense Department nor any of the services are inclined to request repeal:

While women have enabled the services to meet recruiting goals in the volunteer environment, this contribution has come at a cost of (1) driving military planners toward assignment decisions that they might not ordinarily make and (2) possibly adversely affecting military morale and readiness. Women are, on the average, smaller and not as strong as men; they have a higher rate of first-term turnover; and they take more time off from duty for medical reasons (though less than men for substance abuse and disciplinary reasons).

It would seem, then, that there are military reasons for excluding women not only from combat but from military service, despite the Pentagon's pro-integration propaganda.

Until recently, the services themselves admitted that the presence of women causes many unresolved problems. Indeed, most of our knowledge of those problems comes from the services' own studies. Thanks to the services, we know that, by most measures, women are a bad buy for the military. They suffer higher rates of attrition and lower rates of retention. They are three times more likely to be discharged for homosexuality. They miss more than twice as much duty time for medical reasons. They are four times more likely to complain of spurious physical ailments. When men and women are subjected to equally demanding physical regimens, the injury rates of women can be as high as fourteen times that of men.

In the course of a year, 10 to 17 percent of all servicewomen will be pregnant. At any one time, 5 to 10 percent of all servicewomen are pregnant, though small units have at times reported pregnancy rates as high as 50 percent. Servicewomen are eight times more likely to be single-parents than men. Though at one time, single-parents were routinely discharged for the good of the service, the services must now expend extraordinary efforts to accommodate their presence, the "protected" status of military women having been extended to all single-parents.

Servicewomen have led repeated assaults against traditional bans on fraternization between persons of different ranks. They also have forced the services to accommodate a growing number of "dual service" marriages, which complicate assignment systems and force the services to sacrifice the efficient use of individual service members to the domestic needs of the more than 56,000 such couples already in service.

Physical limitations make it impossible for most women to live up to the boast that they are performing as well as or better than men. Contrary to popular belief, technology has not relieved service members of the need for above-average physical strength. A 1982 Army study found that barely one tenth of Army women possessed the strength to meet minimum physical requirements for 75 percent of the jobs for Army enlisted personnel, yet half of the Army's enlisted women were assigned to those jobs. In 1985, the Navy found that a predominantly female fire-fighting unit at a naval station in Alaska required a 25 percent increase in personnel to make up for the lack of physical strength among female fire-fighters.

Psychological Differences

The services have also documented psychological differences that make women less effective members of the military. Military women are less aggressive, less daring, less likely to suppress minor personal hurts, less aware of world affairs, less interested in military history, less respectful of military tradition, and less inclined to make the military a career. They are more likely to suffer emotional distress as a result of changes in their lives and are better suited for routine, sedentary duties. They score lower than men on entrance exams in those subjects most relevant to the majority of modern military jobs. They overwhelmingly prefer traditionally female jobs and pleasant working environments. Women steered by recruiters into traditionally male jobs suffer higher rates of attrition and tend to migrate into traditionally female jobs.

Women offer the services one single advantage over men: they are better behaved. They lose less time for disciplinary reasons and are less prone to drug and alcohol abuse. They are also more likely to have completed high school before entry, but high school completion is only significant as an indication that a recruit will complete an enlistment contract. Because women are less likely to stay in the military, the fact that women are more likely to have completed high school hardly matters.

Public Support

None of these problems are unknown to the nation's top military leaders, who, despite their public support for sexual equality in the military, are not clamoring for more women. The fears of military women that the services are insincere in their support for integration are well-founded. In truth, the services would rather have men if they could get them. They put up with women for two reasons: first, most of them believe that the success of the All-Volunteer Force depends upon the use of women, and second, politics gives them little say in the matter.

The merit of the first reason is debatable. The AVF was never allowed to work without women. At the start, its architects resorted to greater use of women without considering the possibility that an all-male military, with its distinctly masculine appeal, might attract more young men than a more feminine force.

The merit of the second reason is undeniable. Pressure from feminists in and out of the federal government has made resisting the march toward full sexual equality in the military suicidal for defense officials. Twice each year, the Defense Advisory Committee on Women in the Services, or DACOWITS, meets to oversee the progress of the march. High-ranking service representatives appear before the mostly female committee like popup targets absorbing the committee's fire on behalf of their service. Their primary concern is to avoid angering the committee. They praise military women effusively and dare not confront the committee with any of the problems just mentioned. Their mission is to keep the committee and its Praetorian guard of active and retired military women from appealing directly to the Secretary of Defense or elevating the dispute to the House Armed Services Committee.

Under present conditions, it is impossible to trust what defense officials tell us about women in the military because they testify under duress.

Different Standards

Even so, we know that much of what they tell us about women in the military is not true. It is not true, for instance, that military women are meeting the same standards as men. In fact, women enjoy preference and protection in a variety of forms. Nowhere are women required to meet the same physical standards as men, and nowhere are women subjected to the military's sternest trials of mind and body that many men face. Pregnancy remains the only "temporary disability" that gives a service member the option of breaking a service contract without penalty. It is also the only disability for which service members cannot be punished for deliberately inflicting upon themselves.

It is not true that the presence of women has had only a positive effect on morale and readiness. Instead, the effect of their presence has been a general softening of military service. Conditions and performance requirements that aggravate attrition among women and expose their limited abilities have been systematically eliminated. . . .

The integration of women has also threatened the very values upon which all militaries depend. Civilized militaries are necessarily hierarchical, anti-egalitarian, and altruistic (in that they exist to serve not themselves but the state). The campaign to win approval of women in the military has argued against the institutional values behind all of these qualities. Proponents of women in the military have founded their arguments on the absolute equality of all persons, they have pitted the rights of individuals against the authority of the hierarchy, and they have encouraged military women to think of themselves and their careers before thinking of the good of the organization and of national defense. Forced to adopt those arguments to defend the task of integration, the services now excuse and even condone among women what they would reprove as selfish careerism among men.

The Defense Department has moved to squelch dissent on the issue and labored to ensure that only the approved view of women in the military is presented to the American people. In so doing, it has fostered cynicism and resentment among military men whose intelligence, integrity, and trust is too often abused by the deceitfulness of those charged with making integration work. At times, the integrators resort to sophistry and newspeak. Cadets at West Point are told that separate standards for women are "dual standards," not double standards. Eliminating tasks too difficult for women is described as "normalizing requirements" to avoid the embarrassing admission that standards have been lowered. At other times, the integrators simply hide the facts. The Defense Department frequently insists that single-parenthood is not a "female problem," pointing to its own statistics which show that three quarters of all military single-parents are men. It does not explain that most men counted as single-parents are actually divorced parents without custody of their children.

A Fundamental Difference

Men are more aggressive by nature than women. Ironically, before feminists became boosters of female soldiering, they used to argue the same thing.

No amount of gender-neutral child rearing can erase this fundamental difference. Violent criminals are almost exclusively male. Vandals, brawlers, and classroom bullies are overwhelmingly male. Even the carefully pacified little boys of earnest feminist psychologists prefer, when permitted, to play with guns.

An argument can be made that women are superior in this sense. Perhaps. But when my country is in danger, I want those inferior males on the front lines.

Mona Charen, *Conservative Chronicle*, April 25, 1990.

The feminization of the American military is perhaps the greatest peacetime military deception ever perpetrated. It continues today to mask the drive toward full sexual equality in the military, which will only be achieved when women are no longer barred from combat and when the numbers of women in the military match the numbers of men.

We are closer than most anyone imagines to both events. Today, the combat exclusions have been sliced so thin that they no longer keep women out of combat but only arbitrarily out of some combat jobs. The very arbitrariness of the exclusions makes them not likely to withstand the next challenge in the courts. The danger to all American women is that their exemption from the military draft depends upon the combat exclusions. When the Supreme Court upheld draft exemptions for women in 1981, it cited the combat exclusions as the only legal grounds for doing so. If the exclusions fall, the draft exemption will find no support in the courts. In the coming battle over the combat exclusions, the American people are on their own. The Defense Department's official non-position on women in combat means that the military will take no part in the battle, except to bear witness to the official view of the record of women in the military so far.

"It is often said that modern technology has erased the physical advantage men have brought to war. This is fantasy."

Women Cannot Fight as Effectively as Men

Lou Marano

Allowing women to serve in combat will threaten the safety of the United States because women cannot fight as well as men, Lou Marano asserts in the following viewpoint. Marano believes that women are physically weaker than men, and that the presence of women in battle will distract men. The goal of the military is to defend the nation, the author states, not to promote the military careers of individual women. Marano, a Vietnam War veteran, is a member of the editorial staff of *The Washington Post*.

As you read, consider the following questions:

1. What does Marano see as the short-term benefits of putting women in combat?
2. Why does the author believe that modern technology will not erase the physical advantage men have in battle?
3. What example does Marano cite to substantiate his belief that women will sexually distract men in battle?

Lou Marano, "Those Who Will Do the Fighting," *The Washington Post*, January 12, 1991, © 1991 The Washington Post. Reprinted with permission.

A consensus has begun to emerge that women should be allowed to serve in combat units if they want to. A recent New York Times/CBS News poll says that seven out of 10 Americans now hold this view.

I respect and admire women who want to serve, but I believe an expanded role for women in the U.S. armed forces is a demonstrably bad idea.

Mine is an unusual perspective. I am a Vietnam veteran, a social scientist and a journalist who has done some reporting on the military. In 1967 and 1968 I was a junior officer in a Seabee battalion that provided construction support to the 3rd Marine Division near the demilitarized zone separating the two Vietnams. Until 1984, I was an anthropology professor who tried to teach his students to understand why cultures develop the way they do and that history is not just the story of one damn thing after another.

Men Fight Better

The simple truth is this: However well one woman (or 1,000 women) may have performed in a firefight in Panama, it does not change the fact that men—as a group—fight better than women. This fact is as unremarkable (and as unsexist) as saying that young men usually make better soldiers than do men who arc no longcr young. All othcr things being equal, an army whose average age is 26 will beat an army whose average age is 46. All other things being equal, an army of men will beat an army of women. All other things being equal, a society that puts women in the field at the expense of fielding a like number of men will lose its wars.

Of course, all other things are never equal. This is why the United States can probably get away for a long time with its policy of using an increasing number of women volunteers to make up for the men who fail to enlist or for Congress's failure to conscript them. Diminishing East-West tensions make a major war seem less likely. Defense cuts, including cuts in personnel, appear inevitable. Since our forces will be smaller anyway, why not let motivated women do as much of the job as they can handle? Isn't it unfair to exclude military women from the most career-enhancing assignments?

Different things are at stake in the short and long terms. I taught my anthropology students that taboos (such as the incest taboo) evolve when the benefits of a contemplated action are immediate and obvious but the costs are veiled and postponed. For untold millennia, every society of which I am aware has had a taboo against sending women to fight while able-bodied men were still available. Now we are on the verge of violating this taboo. Before we embrace the violation as our national policy, we should consider the consequences.

The short-term benefits are clear. Americans prize autonomy of the individual. That's what we fought for in past wars, isn't it? Women now make up almost 11 percent of the armed forces. Why exclude them from combat only to replace them with men less eager? The United States may be entering an era of brush-fire wars and relatively small regional conflicts that present no immediate threat to the survival of the nation. America is still a vast, rich country that will continue to hold a huge advantage in resources, population and technology over any probable combination of enemies. Under these circumstances an expanded military role for women could cause serious problems, perhaps even defeat, but would not result in the conquest of the United States by foreign powers.

Men Make Better Fighters

The high-intensity, limited warfare of the future will not resemble a computer-game arcade. Digging a 4-ft. foxhole in 30 minutes, sticking a bayonet in an enemy's midsection, or doing a forced 20-mile march, with full pack (our soldiers typically go into battle carrying 75 pounds of gear) will not be enhanced by that "sensitive touch."

Only by deliberately disregarding reality can one conclude that the sexes are equally adept at soldiering. Women have 55 percent of the muscular strength and 67 percent of the endurance of men. Feminist psychologists Carol Jacklin and Eleanor Maccoby, in their book *The Psychology of Sex Differences*, conclude that men are naturally more aggressive, more driven to dominate and lead than women.

Don Feder, *Conservative Chronicle*, April 25, 1990.

The long-term costs are hidden but deadly. One way to think about these costs is to consider the "law of the minimum," propounded by Justus von Liebig, a 19th century German chemist and a pioneer in agricultural research. He discovered that plant growth is limited if one necessary factor is unavailable—even if all the other factors are available in abundance. Applied to human societies, Liebig's "law of the minimum" suggests that survival is not geared to coping with good conditions, or even to average conditions, but to an ability to get through the worst crises.

Militarily, that worst crisis is total war, which has come to the world twice in this century. Both times America got off easy in the expenditures of one necessary factor: manpower.

Unlike Europe, the United States never fully mobilized its population for military service. Even during World War II, we didn't push up against Liebig's law of the minimum. On Sept. 20, 1943, Gen. George C. Marshall testified before the Senate against a bill that would have deferred from the draft men who were fathers before Pearl Harbor. Similar bills would have been laughed out of the legislatures of the European powers.

Take a look at photographs of soldiers in the European armies of both world wars. You will see faces of many older men, many of them fathers. Still, they did not draft women. And with the exception of the Soviet Union, which ran out of men in World War II, they didn't push women toward combat. There are two good reasons for this: Men generally fight better than women, and men generally fight better when women aren't around.

The Israeli Example

A misunderstanding of the Israeli example clouds the issue. Contrary to popular belief, Israel does not conscript women to fight—and certainly not so that able-bodied men can be excused from military service—but to free men to fight in combat units. Israelis I've talked to think that the U.S. trend of allowing women to enter combat situations is folly.

It is often said that modern technology has erased the physical advantage men have brought to war. This is fantasy. It is not even true in support units. I recall several occasions in Vietnam when I grew faint after manhandling (good word, that) ammunition crates or sandbags for hours in the blinding heat. The point is not that some women could have done better; it is that most women could not have done as well.

It is also said that sexual distraction in military life is an issue only for relics like me, and that today's more enlightened generation of young men develop nothing but brotherly affection for their female "buddies." Not only does this go against all experience and common sense, but I found it to be false when reporting on U.S. forces deployed to the mountains of Honduras in 1988. While frustration, heartbreak and jealousy did not seem to be problems for the Army reservists and National Guard members who came into the camp and returned to the United States after a few weeks, they certainly were present among the sexually mixed camp cadre, who had to live with each other for almost a year. Human nature doesn't change, and we are asking for trouble by pretending it has.

Mission Comes First

It was drilled into my head when I was on active duty that the mission came first and the welfare of the people I led came second. Aren't those who promote equal opportunity for women in combat violating that most basic principle of military leader-

85

ship? What's good for individual careers isn't necessarily good for the country. The mission of the armed forces is to win wars, not under the best conditions or average conditions but with a margin for error under worse conditions than can be imagined. In a crisis, the country that puts women in the field at the expense of men will lose. Meeting such a crisis successfully is never easy, and it may become impossible if our culture changes to the point where American men are no longer embarrassed to have women do their fighting for them.

"Strength testing and other physical requirements have a potential for unnecessarily excluding and limiting women."

Women Can Fight as Effectively as Men

Judith Hicks Stiehm

Judith Hicks Stiehm is the provost of Florida International University in Miami and the author of several books, including *Bring Me Men and Women: Mandated Change at the U.S. Air Force Academy* and *Arms and the Enlisted Woman,* from which the following viewpoint is excerpted. Stiehm argues that women are strong enough to fight effectively. She contends that the military uses physical strength tests as a way to exclude women, not as a legitimate measure of a soldier's ability. The military should redesign tests and equipment to meet women's needs, the author argues, rather than exclude women on the basis of physical strength.

As you read, consider the following questions:

1. What two reasons does the author give to explain why physical strength is now a topic of debate in the military?
2. Some experts contend that the smaller stature of women prevents them from being competent soldiers. Why does Stiehm question the seriousness of this criticism?
3. How is the Marine Corps different from the other military services in its approach to physical strength requirements, according to the author?

When civilians with unformed opinions about women in the military first begin to think about the subject, they often begin with biology. They question women's capacity, their fitness and strength; they ponder the meaning of sex between soldiers; and they reflect upon military families—particularly those in which mothers and wives wear uniforms.

Fitness is a concern both at the time of enlistment and during service. Establishing physical standards for enlistment has proven relatively easy and noncontroversial; establishing and, especially, enforcing standards for continuing service have been more problematic. Physical strength has become an issue only recently as women have (1) moved into jobs that require heavy work and into previously all-male units, and (2) become a significant proportion of the personnel in particular units and specialties. . . .

Questions About Women's Participation

The Army has long considered the problem of physical strength in estimating just how many women it can "utilize." A 1958 study concluded that 25 percent of the Army could be female, using the same criteria that are used today—physical strength and relation to combat. To arrive at this number, the 1958 study estimated that fewer than 25 percent of its MOSs [military occupational specialties] required lifting and carrying fifty pounds as part of the serviceperson's regular duties; it prescribed no strength testing for either women or men. By the late 1970s, however, discussion inside the Army about the utility and utilization of women was vigorous. Questions about the effect of women's participation on Soviet perceptions of U.S. strength, on unit morale, and on civilian support for the military excited strong feelings. At least one memo said, "The Army should take no more women." Strong as these views were, they did not prevail—at least not immediately and directly. What would make it possible for the Army to "take no more women"—to hold the number of women in the Army constant in 1980—was the development of a new rationale for restrictions. . . .

A Serious Problem?

Physical-strength testing was begun in 1984. In effect, the Army had two clusters—"light" and "heavy." Over 99 percent of men and 21 percent of women were able to lift 80 pounds, thus qualifying for "heavy" work. Most of the new male recruits took heavy jobs, but 17 percent of those eligible for heavy jobs took light ones. Women eligible for heavy jobs divided about equally between heavy and light; however, almost a third of the women eligible for only light work actually took heavy jobs. In absolute numbers, more than 40,000 men and 3,000 women took heavy jobs. Some 8,700 men and 5,300 women took light jobs.

Cutoff scores for mental qualification are regularly varied; the military wishes to get "enough" draftees or enlistees and does so. The same thing will surely occur with physical standards, but when the categories are large and the tests skip from 50- to 80- to 100-pound lifts, adjustments will be both more difficult and more visible than they are for changes in mental standards, and may be perceived as more compromising. At the same time, questions about scaling equipment and tasks to women's size have gone almost unaddressed. U.S. forces regularly share equipment with men of other nations whose size and strength are significantly less than that of U.S. personnel. This leads one to wonder how serious the problem really is, since no literature has appeared to suggest that small allies (as contrasted with women) create any difficulty.

A Fighting Spirit

When the first armies were formed, the course of battle took courage, which women share equally with men, and strength, which we do not.

But though I am only 4 feet 7 inches tall, with a gun in my hand I am the equal of a soldier who's 6 feet 7—and perhaps even at a slight advantage, as I make a smaller target.

This is not to say hand-to-hand fighting is a thing of the past, but it is no longer the predominant method. That a general would want the biggest, strongest men in the front lines goes without question, but it is also true that women could fill many, many other roles—from driving a tank to dropping a bomb to firing a cannon to acting as snipers. A fighting spirit is the most important ingredient in the makeup of a fighter.

Ruth Westheimer, *The New York Times*, February 10, 1990.

Moreover, the U.S. population is becoming more ethnically diverse, and different groups have different average heights and weights. Does the Army really want, for instance, to have men of Asian or Latin descent concentrated in particular types of jobs because of size and strength measures? Or do the Army and the country want all male citizens available for any assignment? During World War II, Japanese Americans were used as fighting men; Sen. Daniel Inouye has described himself at five feet, six inches as a big man in his unit and noted that some of his men wore size-four shoes! In the past and even now, the military seems to have been able to accommodate men of many sizes. Physical strength has not been an issue. Individuals were simply used as needed. The real issue, then, seems to be extending the range of size (and strength) to include *women*, not extending the range per se.

Strength has never been a criterion for men's participation except in certain elite units. It is not clear that the Army really wants to use it as a criterion for men, because a crucial element of military service is fairness, and "fairness" is usually taken to mean inclusiveness—equal risk. Further, no one seems to have analyzed how less physical strength might be balanced by the other desirable qualities (e.g., education) an enlistee might offer. It is almost as though physical-strength testing is being used to reduce opportunities for women in an "objective," "gender-free" way because women are a problem, not because strength is a problem.

Finally, if the Army wishes to utilize fully the available pool of personnel, should it not reserve the "light," "medium," and "moderately heavy" jobs for people who cannot meet higher standards? This would mean that about a quarter of the Army's jobs would be reserved for the 74 percent of women and 0 percent of men ineligible for heavier jobs. Competition for jobs would then be more balanced, although over a third of the youth pool would still be competing for a quarter of the jobs. Certain MOSs might become all or mostly female if this were done but all-female units have not been an obvious disservice to the Army—consider, for example, the Army Nurse Corps.

No Tests of Competence

One study the Army did *not* undertake was to see how women who could not pass the proposed physical-strength test were doing in their jobs. Were the estimated requirements valid? Or have women found ways to do the work? The Army analysts found five jobs rated "heavy" or "very heavy" that had substantial numbers of women working in them. In these cases the Army actually redefined ("separated") the MOS to remove the onerous duties from the job description. Thus, the Army made women more likely to qualify for the jobs they were already in: wire systems installer/operator, ammunition specialist, motor transport operator, medical specialist, and military police.

The Marine Corps has taken an entirely different approach to the question of strength. It considers basic training its physical-standards test: if one can get through basic, one is fit to be a Marine. The Marine Corps claims to wonder exactly what other services' "basic" is all about if large numbers of women and men can pass it and still not be able to do the services' jobs. . . .

Achieving physical fitness is not a special problem for women. Particular training programs and the spirit in which they are conducted can have different consequences for morale, but separate standards are set for women and men, and most are able to meet those standards.

Physical strength is another matter. The debate is not (or should not be) over how strong women are, but over how strong they need to be. Strength testing and other physical requirements have a potential for unnecessarily excluding and limiting women and doing so with an aura of objectivity and certainty that is hard to counter. . . .

The Air Force is now studying how much strength is needed to be a pilot. One can confidently predict that if the study is ever released, it will show that a substantial number of women are not strong enough to be pilots. One can also predict that if women were the purchasers and intended operators of military planes, manufacturers would design them so that 100 percent of women would have the strength to fly. It is merely a matter of design and market. Unfortunately, there is almost no evidence that any of the services are serious about redesigning physically demanding equipment for women's use.

Recognizing Stereotypes

A stereotype is an oversimplified or exaggerated description of people or things. Stereotyping can be favorable. Most stereotyping, however, tends to be highly uncomplimentary and, at times, degrading.

Stereotyping grows out of our prejudices. When we stereotype someone, we are prejudging him or her. Consider the following example: Mr. Smith believes all women are physically incapable of doing many of the activities men do. For example, if he sees a woman whose car has a flat tire, he assumes that she is too weak to change the tire herself and determines that she needs the help of a man. He disregards the fact that many women are as capable as men at changing tires. Because of his stereotype, Mr. Smith labels all women as weak and helpless. He has prejudged all women and will keep his stereotype consistent with his prejudice.

Part I

The following statements relate to the subject matter in this chapter. Consider each statement carefully. *Mark S for any statement that is an example of stereotyping. Mark N for any statement that is not an example of stereotyping. Mark U if you are undecided about any statement.*

S = *stereotype*
N = *not a stereotype*
U = *undecided*

1. Men are more aggressive than women.

2. Female soldiers are not as qualified as their male counterparts.

3. Women lose less time from their jobs for reasons of illness or disability than do men.

4. The average woman is shorter than the average man.

5. The presence of women in the military undermines the effectiveness of military men.

6. Female soldiers are lesbians.

7. Women have a physical advantage in some types of warfare.

8. Women are weaker than men.

9. Male soldiers do not show their emotions.

10. Men do not want women in the army.

11. Men's natural aggressiveness is necessary to success in battle.

12. Military women are less aggressive and less daring than men.

13. Women are nurturers who excel at taking care of children.

14. Men outnumber women in the U.S. military.

15. Women are three times more likely to be discharged for homosexuality than men.

16. Women are sensitive to the feelings of others.

17. Women soldiers need less disciplining and are less prone to drug and alcohol abuse than male soldiers.

18. Women are more likely than men to have completed high school before entering the military.

19. Because men only think about sex, they are easily distracted by women soldiers.

Part II

Based on the insights you have gained from this activity, discuss these questions in class:

1. Why do people stereotype one another?

2. What are some examples of positive stereotypes?

3. What harm can stereotypes cause?

4. What stereotypes currently affect members of your class?

Periodical Bibliography

The following articles have been selected to supplement the diverse views presented in this chapter.

Clare Ansberry and Carol Hymowitz	"Gulf War Takes a Toll on Soldiers' Children," *The Wall Street Journal,* January 29, 1991.
Carol Barkalow	"Women Really Are an Integral Part of the Military," *Army Times,* May 27, 1991. Available from Springfield, VA 22159.
Melinda Beck et al.	"Our Women in the Desert," *Newsweek,* September 10, 1990.
James G. Bruen Jr.	"Women at War with Themselves," *Fidelity,* October 1990. Available from 206 Marquette Ave., South Bend, IN 46617.
Elaine Donnelly	"Should We Have Mothers in the Military?" *Human Events,* March 16, 1991. Available from 4422 First St. SE, Washington, DC 20003.
Lorraine Dusky	"Combat Ban Stops Women's Progress, Not Bullets," *McCall's,* May 1990.
Alice Fleming	"Women: Their Changing Military Role," *The American Legion Magazine,* March 1990.
Anne Gowen	"Soldiers, Gender, and 'Warmones,'" *Insight,* March 4, 1991. Available from PO Box 91022, Washington, DC 20090-1022.
Barbara Grizzuti Harrison	"Should Women Have the Right to Fight?" *Mademoiselle,* June 1990.
Brian Mitchell and Molly Yard	"Should Military Women Serve in Combat?" *The American Legion Magazine,* May 1990.
People Weekly	"A Mother's Duty," September 10, 1990.
Michael Ryan	"A Woman's Place Is at the Front," *People Weekly,* January 22, 1990.
Phyllis Schlafly	"Sending Mothers to the Gulf War!" *The Phyllis Schlafly Report,* March 1991. Available from PO Box 618, Alton, IL 62002.
Jean Yarbrough	"The Feminist Mistake: Sexual Equality and the Decline of the American Military," *Policy Review,* Summer 1985.

3 CHAPTER

Should Defense Spending Be Decreased?

AMERICA'S DEFENSE

Chapter Preface

In January 1991, U.S. and allied military forces attacked Iraqi forces who had seized Kuwait six months earlier. This war, which came to be known as the Persian Gulf War, was quick and decisive. By the middle of March, America and its allies had pushed the Iraqis out of Kuwait while suffering relatively few casualties. The Iraqis, by contrast, lost at least ten thousand men.

Many military analysts believe that the U.S. victory over Iraq vindicates those who supported the increases in defense spending made during the Reagan administration. These experts hypothesize that if the U.S. had not increased defense spending during the 1980s, it would have been incapable of defeating Iraq so swiftly, if at all. Such experts favor increasing defense spending or maintaining it at the 1991 level of $273 billion. They warn that cuts in defense could threaten the safety of the U.S. One such expert, Frank J. Gaffney Jr., the director of the Center for Security Policy, maintains, "If planned Pentagon cuts are fully implemented, by 1995 the United States would not be able to mount a Desert Storm operation." Gaffney and others oppose plans to reduce the military to 536,000 soldiers by 1995. Military staffing specialist Charles C. Moskos believes such a military would be "a small expeditionary force with little staying power," inadequate to defend America and its allies.

Ironically, opponents of increased defense spending also cite the Persian Gulf victory to support their view that the U.S. is more than adequately defended. The Center for Defense Information, a Washington, D.C., think tank, points out that the U.S. was able to defeat Iraq using only 17 percent of U.S. active and reserve personnel and approximately one-third of its major combat units. The Center and other opponents of increased defense spending conclude that the U.S. could easily cut the military budget and still maintain a strong military. As Massachusetts Democrat Barney Frank, a member of the U.S. House of Representatives, states, "Given . . . America's proven military superiority over any likely adversary, a military budget that is less than two-thirds of our current expenditure would more than suffice to keep us the strongest power in the world."

How much money the U.S. military needs to satisfactorily defend the nation is a contentious issue made more so by the victory in the Persian Gulf. The following chapter presents a variety of views concerning this topic.

"The defense budget could be cut in half over ten years and still leave the United States and its allies secure."

Defense Spending Should Be Decreased

Jeff Faux and Max Sawicky

For many years, the primary goal of the U.S. military was to deter the Soviet Union from attacking the U.S. and Western Europe. To accomplish this goal, the U.S. increased military spending. Since the end of the Cold War, however, many experts contend that the Soviet threat no longer exists and that the United States no longer needs such a large defense budget. In the following viewpoint, Jeff Faux and Max Sawicky agree with this position and argue that the U.S. can now safely cut its defense spending by at least 50 percent. Faux and Sawicky maintain that the money saved from cutting defense spending could be used to strengthen America's economy. Faux is the president of the Economic Policy Institute, a nonprofit research think tank in Washington, D.C. Sawicky is an economist for the institute.

As you read, consider the following questions:

1. What do the authors believe is the most important question to ask when evaluating America's defense spending?
2. Why do Faux and Sawicky believe the military threat once posed by the Soviets will never reappear?
3. How can the U.S. find new uses for the labor and capital currently invested in the defense industry, in the authors' opinion?

Adapted from "Investing the Peace Dividend: How to Break the Gramm-Rudman-Hollings Stalemate," by Jeff Faux and Max Sawicky, 1990. Reprinted with permission.

97

The cold war is over. There is simply no rationale for a defense budget of the size now contemplated by the Bush administration. One need not be an expert in military strategy or international affairs to understand that spending anywhere near $300 billion on defense in Fiscal Year (FY) 1991 is an irresponsible waste of money.

The administration's budget proposes that it be given the authority in FY 1991 to commit $307 billion to be spent for military purposes. Actual spending would be about $303 billion, representing a 2.3 percent increase in nominal terms, which an assumed 4.9 percent inflation rate translates into a 2.6 percent cut in real terms. This budget provides for only a slight change in the rate of decline since the defense budget peak of FY 1987; in real terms that decline has averaged 2 percent per year in spending and 2.9 percent per year in budgetary authority. Given the dramatic change in the international political climate, Bush's budget is completely isolated from reality.

How Much to Spend?

The first step in bringing the military budget in sync with the world as it now exists is to ask the right question. Before determining how much we can *cut* from the present budget, we first must ask: "How much do we need to spend?" Prevailing practice takes the present budget as a point of departure, making what we did yesterday the principal yardstick for judging what we should do tomorrow. It is ironically reminiscent of the bureaucratic planning style that has failed in Eastern Europe. If, on the other hand, we begin by determining what we *need* to spend, we have a chance to separate actual defense considerations from the financial interests and bureaucratic inertia that stand in the way of a rational defense budget.

One place to begin is with the lowest level of spending in real dollars. By this measure, as recently as 1976 under a Republican president, when a united Warsaw Pact was armed to the teeth, the U.S. defense budget was $203 billion in 1990 dollars. It is impossible to take seriously the argument that under present conditions—when the Warsaw Pact is irrelevant, the Berlin Wall obliterated, Germany is unified, democratic and economic reforms sweeping the Soviet Union, and international communism virtually eliminated as a force in the world—we need to spend more, in real terms, than we did in 1976.

If we answer the question of how much we need from the "bottom up"—from an analysis of the minimum necessary weapons systems and troop deployments to defend our interests—we get an even smaller figure. Several expert studies—by former DOD (Department of Defense) official William Kaufmann, by the World Policy Institute (WPI), and by a group headed by former Assistant Secretary of Defense Lawrence Korb and former CIA [Central Intelligence Agency] Director William Colby—have shown that the defense budget could be cut in half over ten years and still leave the United States and its allies secure. A number of other experts, including former Defense Secretaries Robert McNamara and James Schlesinger, have supported the general thrust of these studies.

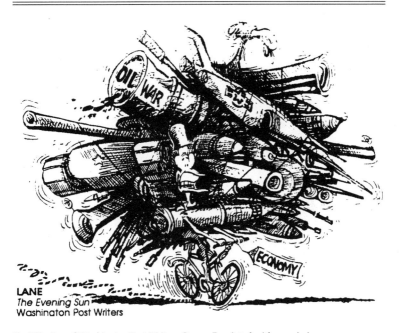

By Mike Lane © Washington Post Writers Group. Reprinted with permission.

These defense reduction plans are based on similar strategic considerations: (1) maintaining a second-strike capability of between three thousand and four thousand submarine- and bomber-launched nuclear warheads, (2) reducing troops and eliminating battlefield nuclear weapons in Europe, (3) maintaining flexible, mobile forces capable of being deployed around the world, and (4) continuing research on new weapons technology.

The studies differ somewhat on what the composition of defense would look like after the reductions. Kaufmann and the Korb group would maintain a sizeable number of troops in Europe and a smaller navy than the WPI group, for example. But the important point is the agreement—among many people who themselves were major players in the buildup of U.S. military power during the cold war—that the United States would be left with a formidable capacity for deploying military force at half the current price.

Thus, whether looked at in aggregate or in terms of specific weapons systems, the financial cost of national security has declined dramatically. *A peace dividend of between $100 and $150 billion already exists. The president's budget, however, proposes that it be spent on the Pentagon.*

Obsolete Negotiations

On the national security side, several arguments on behalf of caution have been advanced:

1. The United States should not reduce its strategic arsenal without corresponding reductions on the Soviet side. We should wait for successful conclusions to the START [Strategic Arms Reduction Talks] negotiations which might not be completed for four or five years.

The current negotiating framework is obsolete. The START talks, for example, were intended to ratify unlimited modernization on both sides in exchange for the destruction of existing warheads. But there is no point in modernizing forces already vastly inflated beyond current needs, particularly at a time when the Soviets are desperate to reduce their defense commitment. Nuclear deterrence was aimed at preventing a Soviet attack on ourselves or our allies in Europe. Events since the fall of 1989 have made it clear that the probabilities of either event are now about zero.

2. The United States should not withdraw from Europe without corresponding reductions by the Soviet side and should maintain some forces there indefinitely for the stability of Europe, entirely apart from the Soviet presence.

The case for delay here is even weaker. [Soviet president Mikhail] Gorbachev has already made unilateral cuts in Soviet conventional forces and, in effect, has been forced to undergo a fifty-five-division cut in the de facto collapse of the Warsaw Pact. And the U.S. battlefield nuclear weapons' range is limited to those nations that are now rapidly aligning with the West.

Nor has a case been made that the United States must now be responsible for European "stability"—a euphemism for fear of German reunification. There is no serious argument that a united Germany is in the foreseeable future a military threat to Europe. The concern is that Europe will be dominated economically—and therefore politically—by the Germans. This may or may not be so. But keeping U.S. troops in Europe will scarcely prevent this; if anything, the drain on our resources will make it easier for the Germans to dominate the United States economically. Many of the European nations have now come close to, and in some cases surpassed, America's levels of per capita wealth and income. With Western European economic integration and the integration of Eastern Europe into a massive market, Europe stands on the brink of extraordinary economic opportunities. We have reached the point where the Europeans themselves must take on the responsibility for sorting out the power balances on that continent.

3. Reductions must proceed very slowly so as to be "reversible" in case Gorbachev should fail and "hardliners" take back control of the Soviet Union.

It is possible that Gorbachev could be overthrown, snuffing out *perestroika* and returning the Soviet Union to totalitarian dictatorship. But whatever happens within the Soviet Union, the military threat that it formerly represented has no significant chance of reappearing in the foreseeable future.

William Webster, director of the U.S. Central Intelligence Agency, has concluded that the contraction of the Soviet Union's offensive military posture is all but irreversible. "Even if a hardline regime were able to regain power in Moscow," he notes, "it would have little incentive to engage in major confrontations with the United States." Moreover, should the cold war return, there will be ample opportunity for the United States to rearm; history has shown that no nation in the world has the ability to gear up to a military economy as quickly as the United States.

One of the best ways to assure the continuation of Gorbachev's revolution is to cut back on U.S. forces threatening the Soviets as quickly as possible. The Soviets are desperate to reduce the burden of armaments on their economy. Delay only strengthens the remaining hardliners in both camps and prevents us from ridding ourselves of a similar burden. Our contribution to the process going on within the Soviet Union is to provide evidence to the Russians that Gorbachev's policies can free up Soviet economic resources without an added threat of military vulnerability to the West.

Domestic Concerns

The second set of rationales for taking as long as a decade to reduce defense spending is domestic. One reasonable concern about the pace of military budget cuts is the impact that such a shift in resource demand might have on the economy. It is conceivable that large and sudden disruptions in important sectors of the economy could endanger the nation's economic growth. But evidence from previous military cutbacks suggests that we can go considerably beyond even the reductions proposed by Kaufmann and the other cited defense analysts (which in turn are far beyond the administration's proposals) before having to worry about the impact on the U.S. economy.

To evaluate the possibility of general decline in economic

growth resulting from military spending cuts, the size of any such cuts should be compared to GNP [gross national product]. U.S. experience provides some guidance. The one-year drop in outlays after the Korean War was as large as 2.2 percent of GNP, which in today's economy would be over $100 billion. This large cut may have helped to produce a short recession in 1954, but largely because the defense cuts were not offset with increases in nondefense public spending. In any event, the economy recovered quickly in 1955 despite the fact that military spending cuts continued.

The largest one-year post-Vietnam cut was 0.9 percent of GNP, the equivalent of almost $50 billion today, and still much larger than anything now being contemplated. But government spending in the aggregate did not decline, and there was no impact on the overall economy.

On the whole, therefore, one-year cuts in defense of less than $50 billion hold no risk of macro-economic harm, unless all or most of it is devoted to fiscal deficit reduction. . . .

The major obstacle in reducing the military budget is the political resistance of those whose economic fortunes will suffer—Pentagon generals, industry executives, politicians from areas with military bases, and anxious workers. This resistance is the administration's high card in the budget game. As Richard Darman has commented, a defense spending cut, "while politically popular in the abstract will not be politically popular in all its particulars."

We cannot, of course, prevent all of the dislocation that will be caused by defense budget reductions. Nor would we want to. The whole point is to "dislocate" resources out of the defense sector. We can, however, do several things to smooth the transition and mitigate the resistance.

Conversion Efforts

The first priority is to make it clear that the military budget will be reduced sharply over the next five years. In the past, expectations (reasonable in view of the historical experience) that the defense business would return created an attitude among contractors of indifference to efforts at conversion.

Given that commitment, defense-conversion efforts should be built around the following principles:

1. Generous severance pay and retraining for affected workers.
2. Economic development planning assistance for affected firms and communities.
3. Establishment of a civilian equivalent of the Defense Advanced Research Projects Agency to begin immediately to finance research and development projects with civilian

payoffs.

4. Identification of "dual use" military technologies with civilian applications (such as high-speed computers, vertical-takeoff aircraft, specialized machine tools), which are now classified or otherwise restricted from commercial development. These technologies would be made available to U.S. companies with, if necessary, government support for long-term financing.

5. Eliminating obsolete cold war restrictions on the export of U.S. commercial equipment to Eastern Europe, which have had the effect of ceding markets to Western European competitors.

Using the peace dividend for domestic investment is the best way to assure that the market will eventually find new uses for labor and capital currently committed to defense production. Even so, temporary periods of unemployment are bound to result. The best way to ease such transition costs is to make a concerted effort to involve communities and defense firms likely to suffer cutbacks in the business of servicing areas where the public budget will be expanding: infrastructure, civilian research and development, and environmental technologies. Here is precisely a case where *planning for conversion* is essential. Indeed, the greatest beneficiary of a shrinkage in the military budget is the economy of the country doing the shrinking. If we are in less danger now than we were in 1976, and if one-half of the military budget is sufficient for our present defense needs, then something less than a ten-year phase down period is clearly in order.

"Before running to the bank with the elusive 'peace dividend,' it would be wise to remember that Soviet military power remains formidable and growing."

Decreases in Defense Spending Could Harm the U.S.

Richard Perle

In the following viewpoint, Richard Perle argues that the Soviets still pose a threat to U.S. security. Consequently, reductions in defense spending could endanger America's safety. Perle maintains that the Soviets are increasing their military spending, and that the U.S. should therefore be extremely cautious in cutting the defense budget. The author believes that a strong U.S. military deterred the Soviets for more than forty years and that continued military strength is necessary to protect the peace. Perle, who was an arms advisor to former U.S. president Ronald Reagan, is a resident fellow with the American Enterprise Institute, a public policy research foundation in Washington, D.C.

As you read, consider the following questions:

1. How did the defense buildup under the Reagan administration help to bring about the end of the Cold War, in the author's opinion?
2. What does Perle anticipate might happen if the U.S. rushes to disarm its military?

Richard Perle, "Dangers of Peace," *The American Legion Magazine,* October 1990. Reprinted by permission, The American Legion Magazine, © 1990.

Early in 1981, the Reagan administration's new leadership at the Pentagon convened a series of top secret meetings in the E-ring conference room of the Secretary of Defense. For several days the most senior Pentagon officials listened to the chiefs of the specified and unified commands, brought back to Washington from their posts around the world. One by one, they described the capacity of the forces under their command to deal with the Soviet threat in their theater.

It was a dismal account indeed. A decade of underinvestment, in which defense spending declined by 3 percent a year in real terms, had caused a multitude of deficiencies. A massive backlog of crucial maintenance; low pay and morale among our men and women in uniform; shortages of tanks, aircraft, missiles and basic munitions; slumbering research and development—this was the picture painted by the men who knew best how ill-prepared we were to meet the challenge of growing military power.

Former Secretary of Defense Harold Brown summarized the 1970s succinctly. Referring to Soviet military spending he said, "When we build, they build. When we stop building, they build."

Reagan's Get-Well Program

The Reagan administration, with strong support in Congress, set about correcting the most glaring deficiencies, rebuilding America's defenses, modernizing our strategic forces, improving the quality of life for our career forces. By and large it was a get-well program. Little in it was new with the important exception of the Strategic Defense Initiative (SDI) launched in the spring of 1983. We resolved not to return to the roller-coaster pattern of defense investment in which we alternated between dangerously low and burdensome high defense budgets.

The Soviets reacted to America's long overdue defense rehabilitation with a massive propaganda campaign. Its principal targets were the strategic modernization program, especially SDI, and the plan to deploy medium range missiles such as Pershing II and ground-launched cruise missiles in Europe.

The restoration of American strength paid a dividend far larger than anyone imagined. It was instrumental in persuading the new Soviet leadership that the achievement of military superiority was beyond the reach of the failing, militarized Soviet economy. It was the decisive factor in bringing the long winter of the Cold War to an end. It was the key to the Western victory in that war.

Now, as we contemplate the need for military power in the aftermath of the Cold War, we must remember that the collapse of the Warsaw Pact, the unraveling of the Soviet empire in Eastern Europe is, in large measure, a result of the postwar strength

and determination of the alliance of Western democracies, led
by the United States. Those who understood the need for nuclear deterrence and serious conventional military capabilities
contributed mightily to the position of strength that eventually
led the Soviet leadership to choose a less bellicose, less menacing approach to international politics.

Ed Gamble. Reprinted with permission.

Now that we see the military power of the Warsaw Pact
ebbing with the receding tide of communist rule and Soviet
domination, there will be those who argue that the Soviet empire never amounted to much, that Western estimates of the
strength of the Warsaw Pact were exaggerated; and that we can
now go shopping for new social programs with the savings the
demise of the Soviet threat will allow us to achieve.

This is of more than passing, historical interest. For it will be
necessary for some time to come to gauge correctly the threat
still posed by Soviet military power in judging how to protect
our security and how to shape our military budget. So, before
running to the bank with the elusive "peace dividend," it would
be wise to remember that Soviet military power remains
formidable and growing even as the Warsaw Pact disintegrates.

Even in their advancing state of decline, the Soviets continue
to spend massively on military power. While we invest about 6

percent of GNP [gross national product] in defense and our allies about 3 percent, the Soviets are spending 25 percent or more, a staggering figure confirmed in 1990 by foreign minister Eduard Shevardnadze in an address to the Soviet Communist Party Congress.

This debilitating Soviet investment in defense, which has proceeded apace despite the absence of any plausible threat, has produced, and continues to produce, a formidable array of military systems, including an aggressive program of nuclear force modernization. Gen. James Gavin put it well when he observed that: "Every month the Soviets still produce enough tanks to outfit an entire division and enough artillery to equip four artillery regiments. Since [Mikhail] Gorbachev assumed power in March 1985, the Soviets have fielded more tanks and artillery pieces than currently exist in the combined armies of Britain, France and West Germany."

Threat No Longer Plausible

The slight slowing observed recently seems to reflect Soviet anticipation of a strategic arms reduction treaty. Even so, it is a slowing that comprehends significant further investment within the levels contemplated by a treaty—if not beyond.

This is not to say that nothing has changed. The transformation of Poland and Hungary, Czechoslovakia and East Germany, Romania and Bulgaria; the tearing down of the Berlin wall; the rising demand in Eastern Europe for a withdrawal of the Soviet troops that kept corrupt and stagnating communist regimes in power against the will of their own citizens; all these changes have profound implications, mostly beneficial, for Western security.

The canonical threat that has dominated our postwar military strategy of a cohesive Warsaw Pact, led by Soviet troops, forcing its way through the center of Europe in a massive invasion of NATO [North Atlantic Treaty Organization] territory, is no longer plausible. But as we consider how to respond, we must take care not to revive that threat by so depleting Western defenses that the advantage once enjoyed by the Warsaw Pact will now belong to the Soviet Union alone.

Extreme proposals that would disarm the West after the Cold War as it was disarmed after World Wars I and II would run the risk that we might yet again make Europe safe for the exertion of Soviet military power. A careless rush to disarm, in which we throw caution to the winds of change, shipping technology and capital to Moscow even as it reels under the weight of a massive military budget; a disregard for the importance of verification of international agreements; a dismantling of Western defenses in ways that would make them difficult or impossible to reconstruct should the need arise—these are the new threats.

Our mission now is to fight an improvident, dangerous euphoria. That should prove easier than preparing to fight the Soviet divisions whose eastward movement we now anticipate celebrating—not so much, by the way, because we've sent an army of diplomats to Vienna, but because the emerging independent nations of Eastern Europe are quite determined to throw them out.

The Nuclear Threat

There is a second threat that is also much diminished. That is the threat of a massive Soviet nuclear strike against the strategic retaliatory forces of the United States—a strike that would entail thousands of nuclear weapons exploding on American territory. In the last few years Soviet attitudes toward nuclear weapons have been evolving away from the contemplation of a massive, disarming strike mounted in peacetime and prepared in secrecy. The days are past when Soviet doctrine considered that nuclear weapons differed little from conventional ones.

This should enable us to reduce the amount we must invest to provide a high degree of deterrence against a massive surprise Soviet nuclear attack. But we can only do that safely if we adopt sensible principles to guide the shaping of a diminished defense budget. And we cannot do it at all, of course, if we now succumb to the siren call of the unilateralists and pacifists whose policies, had we followed them, would have kept the Cold War going or even allowed the Soviet bloc to win it.

The rapidity of recent change should humble us as we make sweeping predictions, although, if experience is any guide, it will spur more people to rashness than it will temper with caution. My vote is for caution as we greet the millennium and divvy up the "peace dividend." That caution has to do with the instability that has resulted from Moscow's loosening grip—not only in Eastern Europe, but in the USSR itself.

Mikhail Gorbachev has set in motion centrifugal forces that have reawakened old ethnic and national allegiances. In Lithuania, Latvia, Estonia, Georgia, Azerbaijan, Moldavia and elsewhere, there are hapless, restive people who have suffered under Soviet imperial domination. They see what is going on in Eastern Europe. They have seen the hammer and sickle torn from national flags; seen statues and regimes toppled, tyrants shot or imprisoned.

No one can say where this will lead. But an unstable Soviet empire could be a dangerous place. We've waited a long time for an opportunity to throw off the burdens of providing security for ourselves and our allies. We would be wise to wait a little longer before confidently predicting that we can afford to be weak in the face of uncertainty.

So how then should we shape the defense budget to take full and creative account of the political changes in Eastern Europe and the beginning of a change in attitude—not yet matched by a change in investment—in the Soviet Union? How can we manage the cuts in defense spending that everyone knows are coming in a way that protects our security while encouraging further change in the Soviet Union?

Two principles should guide the shaping of a national strategy and the defense budget that goes along with it.

•First, we should reduce the force structure to reflect the lessened Warsaw Pact threat while maintaining the quality of the smaller residual force, especially as regards the cadre necessary to re-establish larger forces, should that become necessary.

•Second, we should protect research and development and the defense industrial base so that we can reconstitute advanced military capabilities, should the need arise.

The application of these two principles would mean a cut in overall military forces, especially ground forces, to assure that a smaller armed forces will be adequately equipped, trained and poised for rapid growth, if our hopes for a less menacing Soviet Union should be disappointed.

It may mean foregoing some planned weapons systems now under development on the grounds that the increased risk in the near term of "making do" with the current generation of equipment is manageable while the future is murky. It is this murkiness that so clearly counsels caution.

Some of the new weapons should be continued. The B-2 aircraft is one. So is the Trident II. Neither the Midgetman nor the rail-mobile MX is now essential; the current generation of ICBMs [inter continental ballistic missiles] should prove adequate for the next few years.

The same should hold true for some conventional weapons systems; making do with the current generation should not entail an intolerable risk while we press ahead with R&D [research and development] and develop a better sense of how the world is evolving. A new tactical fighter aircraft should probably be delayed at this moment but it would be wise to develop a future fighter down the road.

Investing in SDI

And there is one program in which we should be investing more rather than less: SDI [Strategic Defense Initiative]. As the prospect of nuclear proliferation draws closer we should be reminded that the threat is neither exclusively Soviet nor, for that matter, exclusively deliberate. There are Third World countries and there are accidents and these two reasons alone would justify a vigorous research and development program to push back even further the frontiers that have recently been yielding to impressive research results. A serious program of R&D reoriented toward limited, partial defenses can and should go forward even in the face of a shrinking defense budget.

The Cold War was won by understanding that the world can be a dangerous place, that national strength is crucial to national security. That war may be over, but the vision that brought us victory will be needed to protect the peace.

"The peace dividend should be used creatively, in ways that build political and social structures for a more humane society."

The Peace Dividend Should Be Spent on Social Programs

S.M. Miller

Those who support decreasing defense spending have suggested that the money once used to deter the Soviets can now be used for nonmilitary purposes. This savings is commonly referred to as the "peace dividend." In the following viewpoint, S.M. Miller proposes that the peace dividend be used to strengthen the U.S. economy, to reduce poverty, and to improve the quality of education. Miller is a professor emeritus of sociology at Boston University in Massachusetts.

As you read, consider the following questions:

1. What three uses for the peace dividend does the author refer to as the "Bush approaches"?
2. What seven steps does Miller believe must be taken for a large peace dividend to be realized?

Excerpted, with permission, from "A Sea Change Around the World" by S.M. Miller, *Social Policy,* Spring 1990. Copyright © 1990 by Social Policy Corporation, New York, New York 10036.

The peace dividend offers a new chance, a new road for the United States. The reordering of the world in the age of *perestroika* and the consequent reductions in "defense" spending can and should reclaim us from our military fixation, the national security state, the *Wehrwirtschaft* (the military economy), and our objective of dominating the world—forces that have so long shackled progressive policies and movements.

One way of perceiving a peace dividend is in narrow financial terms: it provides a chance at money—a scarce commodity for years—to fill the Reagan-promoted social gaps that have worsened the conditions of so many. A broader, more challenging view of the peace dividend and the waning of the Cold War that makes it likely is that it can be the beginning of a new way of thinking about and acting in American society. A broadly conceived peace dividend offers great possibilities for changing the texture of American society—reducing inequalities, shifting national objectives, changing the moral tone—as well as redirecting the flows of governmental spending. . . .

The peace dividend should be a way of rethinking and restructuring the American economy and society. Demilitarizing the economy should also mean demilitarizing American minds. How to use the peace dividend can lead to reshaping American society for the very new conditions it faces of falling behind in international competition and in quality of life. The excesses of greed, selfishness and materialism of the '80s can be challenged as we debate how best to use the peace dividend. . . .

The Making of a Peace Dividend

Recognizing the great potentials of the peace dividend should not lead us to believe that a sizable dividend is a sure thing. It will be a struggle to get a peace dividend that can be decisive. The Bush administration is not only seeking a too-small reduction in military spending, but also seeks to divert the resulting peace dividend to reduction of the federal budget deficit. Its strategy seems to aim at piecemeal uses of the dividend rather than a bold redirection of American goals through new funds. Many view the peace dividend in short-term perspective—handling the burden of foreign aid, say, for Eastern Europe—rather than as part of a long-term process of change. The need is not only for a large but also for a well-used peace dividend. . . .

The political appeal of the uses of the peace dividend affects its size. If the peace dividend is buried in the federal budget or is regarded as dissipated in small, not-very-effective disbursements, then support for it will not grow. A well-used dividend would garner support. How the dividend would be used affects its size; its size affects how well a peace dividend could be used. The need is to offer a program of action that compels support for large spending, the funds for which would come to a major extent from a sizable peace dividend.

The attractions of the peace dividend may be lost in the competition for its uses. The Reagan years have piled up problems. Many economists and businessfolk advocate using the dividend to reduce the federal deficit. That approach seems to have strong support in the Bush administration, at least before the presidential election year of 1992. In the nation, the threat of the budget deficit has receded mightily and the notion is that it has not been as burdensome as anticipated and that it is on the way to gradual reduction. But there will be a pull for using the dividend to reduce the budget deficit.

What Weapons Cost

Item	Cost	Would...
23 Patriot missiles	$22.5 million	Buy 12 months of clothes, seeds, and pots and pay for their storage for 2 million people in Mozambique or cover the Amnesty International Secretariat's 1990 budget
216 Tomahawk cruise missiles	$280.8 million	Buy food needed in Ethiopia for six months
Two F-15E fighter jets	$62.7 million	Nearly equal British Save the Children Fund's overseas budget, 1990-1
One bomb on a B-52	$11,000	Run a clinic for 4,060 patients in Bangladesh for one month or set up a self-running medical supply system for a rural population of 100,000

Source: *The Guardian,* April 1991.

A second use could be for tax reduction, usually very attractive to politicians. Recent public opinion data indicate that sentiment for tax decreases is much less than support for using the peace dividend to deal with pressing social needs. Nonetheless, the Bush administration may push for tax reduction if it loses on its proposal of lowering the capital gains tax.

A third possible use is for foreign aid and other short-term issues. Indeed, this is what the Bush administration has proposed: use the peace dividend to cover the costs of aid to Panama and Nicaragua, possibly to Eastern Europe. These foreign aid proposals, it is to be hoped, will be judged on their own merits and not tied to the dividend.

These three uses—budget and tax reductions and foreign

aid—are the Bush approaches and they have some support. They aim at short-time easing and small political capital. An alternative interpretation is that the administration seeks a small, not very visible peace dividend for the next months and then will reveal a major program for a larger peace dividend in time to benefit in the 1992 presidential and congressional elections. The term "peace dividend" does not describe just one set of proposals, and supporting a peace dividend does not in every case mean supporting a progressive agenda.

Uses of the Peace Dividend

Many moderates join liberals and progressives in seeing two more pressing uses for the peace dividend. One use is to deal with disturbing social needs such as homelessness, addictions, inadequate medical care. Even the editorials of the *New York Times*, once fixated on the imperative of budget deficit reduction, now advocate using the dividend for domestic needs.

The other crucial need is for investment in rebuilding the infrastructure of this country. That underpinning involves both physical and social development. Roads, bridges, transportation systems and the like have to be repaired and extended. Research and development of civilian products and processes should be aided. Most important is investment in people, which should be seen as investment in the economy. A better educated, trained and healthy labor force, childcare for working parents, and decent housing are basic to having a productive economy. Other nations have discovered these prerequisites for effective competition; the US has to make a major jump to catch up. The peace dividend could make possible that advance.

People of very diverse and different outlooks can agree on the importance of dealing with both social needs and investment in the economy. As polls reveal, support for this agenda is considerable. But its enactment is not assured.

Many steps have to be pursued if a large, well-used peace dividend is to be realized. One step is to allay unemployment and dislocation fears arising from military base closings and defense plant shutdowns. Extensive support for communities, factories and workers facing major reductions in direct and indirect Defense Department support is necessary. . . .

Second, unions, minority and women's organizations have to gain an early stake in the struggle for a peace dividend. Their support is important and likely to be secured only if they feel that they have a significant role in the pursuit and allocation of the peace dividend.

Third, the public opinion surveys that demonstrate support for a large peace dividend have to be converted into *targeted* political ammunition. Reluctant members of Congress should be confronted with local surveys and other evidence (e.g., petitions, letters) of widespread and deep support for a large peace dividend in their congressional districts. Representatives who are more positive about the dividend should be encouraged to take leadership roles in gaining legislative action for a large, well-used dividend.

Fourth, support for the peace dividend should be pursued among businesspeople and other elite groups. The peace dividend notion is not a special progressive idea and interest but one that also appeals to a wide range of people who do not have progressive ideological outlooks. The peace dividend is not locked in a political ghetto, a left-right split. Many businesspeople in large and small enterprises recognize that the agony of social needs and underinvestment in the social and physical infrastructure damage the American economy and the long-term prospects of American enterprises. True, they have been reluctant to speak out on the undermining of American society and economy that has been occurring, but it is unlikely that the US will continue to have one of the more shortsighted, narrow business classes in the world while other nations demonstrate that their business leaders know how to think about and adjust to worldwide changes. The strong support of the Marshall Plan demonstrated long-term thinking by business leaders and others. Many in the business elite came to recognize that the Vietnam War was divisive and immoral and became critical of its pursuit. The peace dividend offers another opportunity for them to move beyond the obsession with the quarterly bottom line. The peace dividend movement should make a particular effort to engage business leaders.

A Large Constituency

Fifth, it is not only business leaders who might be brought to support the peace dividend. A majority of Americans indicate dismay about the direction the US is headed and feel something should be done. Some focus on the plight of families and children; others on inner-city minorities; and still others on damages to the environment and daily life. Remedying the threats they recognize requires funds, and the peace dividend offers the best opportunity for action. A potentially large constituency needs to be pulled together.

Sixth, internal wrangling among peace dividend constituencies has to be avoided. If center stage focuses on debates about the distribution between direct social need alleviation and rebuilding the physical and social infrastructures or which acute social need should have priority, the result is likely to reduce prospects for a large peace dividend. Interested parties have to agree fairly soon on a viable and attractive peace dividend, perhaps outlining how the dividend should be used at different money levels.

Seventh, the peace dividend should be used creatively, in ways that build political and social structures for a more humane society. Programs to deal with pressing social needs should not just receive funds that have been withheld from them over the years. Since many supporters have been critical of these programs in the past, the need is to both defend and change these programs, making them more effective, more empowering, more participatory, more efficient. Similarly, the awarding of physical infrastructure contracts should be allocated on the basis of the "best bid," not the lowest bid. "Best bid" weighs how much and what kind of employment (minorities, women, promotion opportunities, training) a contractor would provide and how the construction approach will affect the environment as well as the bid's dollar cost. Worker and community cooperatives, for instance, might get more positive weights than private contractors' bids.

If a large dividend is to be realized, disturbing compromises will be inevitable. This is an unfortunate fact of political life. Not all of the dividend can go to deal with pressing social needs. Some of the dividend will have to go to build support for a large reduction in military spending. Some funds will have to go to conversion and alleviation of the problems of those who lose their jobs because of the military contraction. Some spending on infrastructure and R&D [research and development] will be necessary to widen support.

The political and moral choice is likely to be between a big percentage of a small pie or a smaller percentage of a much larger pie. I am for the latter; it will provide more for social needs and other uses.

New Politics

Some reduction in military spending is going to happen; over time, it could be a considerable sum. What happens is not economically or militarily determined but almost a pure political issue where pressure, mobilization, and widespread evidence of support will count.

To avoid fumbling this great opportunity, we should be beginning on the *new politics* widely recognized as needed today. . . . The peace dividend can provide possibilities for moving in new ways as well as serving as a metaphor for a refocusing away from Cold War economism and moralism. It is an opening that should not be frittered away.

116

"The peace dividend . . . belongs to the American people, who created the wealth in the first place."

The Peace Dividend Should Be Used to Reduce Taxes

Edward H. Crane

Edward H. Crane is the president of the Cato Institute, a public policy think tank in Washington, D.C. In the following viewpoint, Crane argues that the peace dividend—the money once used to deter Soviet aggression—should be returned to the American taxpayers, who have supported a large U.S. military since World War II. Crane concludes that the U.S. government should not spend the peace dividend, but should return it to the taxpayers.

As you read, consider the following questions:

1. To what extent does Crane attribute the success of the private sector?
2. Why does the author believe that a land war in Europe is unlikely?
3. How will lower income taxes affect the U.S. economy, according to the author?

Excerpted, with permission, from *America's Peace Dividend: Income Tax Reductions from the New Strategic Realities* by Edward H. Crane. Washington, DC: Cato Institute, 1990.

President Bush's decision to renege on his oft-stated campaign pledge not to increase taxes on the American people is symptomatic of a broader problem in the nation's capital. Inside the Beltway there is a "culture of spending" in which it is assumed that the legitimate mission of elected officials and senior bureaucrats is to spend other people's money. The deleterious impact of that mistaken notion is compounded by another phenomenon that has been aptly dubbed "the tyranny of the status quo" by Milton and Rose Friedman.

A bill may be debated in Congress for years, or even decades, finally to pass into law by a single vote. From that point forward, however, the only debate is over whether the new program's budget should be increased by 5 or 15 percent. To question whether the program is successful or whether it, god forbid, surpassed the cost estimates of its proponents, is considered a bit gauche. Indeed, the less successful the program, the greater the need (it is typically argued) for additional funds to make it work.

The Clamor for Taxes

All of this has an upward ratcheting effect on federal spending. Taxes, the lifeblood of such spending, are understandably in great favor (even among those who occasionally demur). George Bush, a creature of government, can be assumed to be sensitive to the clamor from inside the Beltway for more taxes. The clamor for lower taxes comes primarily from those outside the Beltway, whose interests are, after all, parochial, if not outright self-serving.

Thus, we are faced with the unseemly prospect of the president of the United States going back on his word (or at least the word of Peggy Noonan, who wrote his "read my lips" speech). Which is not to make light of a very serious problem confronting the American people: the intractability of government interventions, even when they have been thoroughly discredited and clearly demonstrated to be counter to the best interests of the nation, or at least no longer effective in advancing those interests.

The gravity of that problem cannot be overstated. For what makes the so-called private sector in our society healthy, and leads to its growth, is a dynamic process that encompasses choice, feedback, successes, and *failures*. Western economies have thrived relative to Eastern bloc economies precisely because such feedback mechanisms are in place. In 1987, for instance, there were 61,000 business failures in the United States, roughly half of which were businesses that had been started in the previous five years. *That is why resources in the private sector are utilized efficiently—mistakes are punished.*

118

Government, on the other hand, is basically immune to such feedback; like a tumor, it grows unimpeded (to use a pejorative analogy). As noted above, what feedback there is tends to be perverse in its impact: failure is often rewarded. There are very few ways for failed federal programs to go out of business. . . .

Reprinted by permission: Tribune Media Services.

Which brings us to the study at hand. No part of the federal budget has been more isolated from constructive feedback than the activities of the Department of Defense. The annual military budget of the United States (which should be distinguished from the defense budget) is roughly $300 billion. As is the case with deposit insurance and any other major government program, there are powerful vested interests at work to ensure that the $300 billion continues to be spent in much the same manner it has been in the past. A fundamental reassessment of the raison d'etre for military spending, in the view of those interests, must be avoided at all costs. Regrettably, most media coverage of defense issues accepts without question the premises put forward by the defense establishment.

Changed Security Conditions

But the global security conditions that led to the development of our present military budget have changed radically, which should make defending the status quo an extremely difficult undertaking. Yet the Bush administration's response to the changed conditions has been, thus far, mostly cosmetic in nature.

After considering America's legitimate security requirements, we conclude that by 1995 our defense expenditures could be scaled back to approximately $120 billion, compared with the administration's projection of $284.5 billion (both amounts expressed in 1991 dollars). The magnitude of the discrepancy in the two figures quite obviously reflects different premises about the state of the world, in addition to different perceptions of our national security interests. . . .

The post-World War II strategic paradigm had outlived its usefulness long before events in Eastern Europe began to unfold. The reality of nuclear parity and the destructiveness of the weapons at hand draw into question the very idea of extensive land wars, for which a high percentage of Pentagon outlays is earmarked. With the collapse of the Warsaw Pact as a viable military alliance, the prospect of a Central European land war involving the Soviet Union becomes more than a little problematic. With the Soviets concerned more about their imploding economy than visions of empire, the value of our far-flung and prohibitively expensive system of alliances must be brought into question. And yet the defense planners in this administration seem stuck in an obsolete, post-World War II analytical mode. Such bureaucratic inertia—as we've learned from the S&L [savings and loan] debacle—can prove enormously costly to the American taxpayer.

Returning the Wealth to the People

Still, there is much talk in Washington these days of a pending "peace dividend," even if the administration seems determined to stonewall military cuts predicated on new strategic realities. The spenders in both parties in Congress have designs on whatever savings may be generated from the new geopolitical realities. We've taken a different tack—one that in our view should always be taken when a spending reduction is available in the federal budget—and that is to send the money directly back to the American people. The congressional mindset says that once revenues have been extracted from the taxpayer they belong to Congress, regardless of changes in the circumstances that purported to necessitate the revenues in the first place. Our view, to the contrary, is that Americans are grossly overtaxed to finance a myriad of counterproductive domestic programs ranging from entitlements to agribusiness subsidies—quite aside from the savings to be found in the military budget.

The peace dividend, then, belongs to the American people, who created the wealth in the first place. . . .

The savings to an average family filing a joint return would amount to $2,119 in current dollars by 1995, the year our proposal would be fully phased in. The cumulative savings from 1991 through 1995 would amount to $5,549.

By 1995 the reduction in military spending would provide an increase in the personal exemption of $1,450, a reduction of the bottom income tax rate from 15 to 12 percent, of the top rate from 28 to 22 percent, and of the transitional rate from 33 to 27 percent. . . .

Economic activity will increase markedly under the stimulus of tax cuts. Some 2.4 million new jobs will be created under the proposal, and annual private economic output will be about $150 billion greater by 1995. . . .

No More Propitious Time

The federal budget deficit will be reduced by $44.3 billion in 1995 as a result of the increased economic activity caused by major cuts in spending and taxes. (For those who might object to our tax cuts in light of the federal budget deficit, one could also point to the fact that the deficit is today less than half what it was in 1985 as a percentage of gross national product.)

The federal government has a responsibility to spend whatever is needed to ensure our national security. But national security is not necessarily served by redundant weapons stockpiles, an expansive military presence around the world, alliances that might involve the United States in regional disputes of negligible importance to us, or a domestic economy deprived of financial and technological resources. . . .

By calling for spending cuts and tax cuts of a magnitude not often heard inside the Beltway, we offer the prospect of a more secure, prosperous, and competitive America. With the spirit of democratic capitalism sweeping the world, there could be no more propitious time for Americans to regain control of their government and put an end to the tyranny of the status quo.

"The U.S. would be more likely to buy truly necessary weapons if decisions were not distorted by the desire of contractors to make huge profits from government contracts."

The Defense Industry Is Wasteful and Inefficient

Center for Defense Information

Critics of military spending often assert that the defense contractors who supply the U.S. military charge exorbitant prices for ineffective or unnecessary weapons. In the following viewpoint, the Center for Defense Information agrees with this assertion and argues that defense contractors are the reason that the U.S. spends so much on defense. The author contends that contractors bribe government officials and go overbudget when developing weapons. The Center for Defense Information is a Washington, D.C., organization that opposes excessive defense spending.

As you read, consider the following questions:

1. Why was defense spending in the 1980s inefficient and wasteful, in the author's opinion?
2. Why do unqualified companies obtain defense contracts, according to the author?
3. What does the author mean by "goldplating"?

Center for Defense Information, "Wasteful Weapons," *The Defense Monitor,* vol. 18, no. 7, 1989. Reprinted with permission.

The United States weapons industry is the biggest in the world. The Pentagon spends about $6 billion per week and executes about 56,000 contracts per working day. But over the past several decades the weapons bought by the Pentagon have become increasingly unrelated to the nation's military needs.

More and more, the U.S. is buying weapons it does not need and is spending too much for the weapons it does buy. . . .

Money and the Military

Since the 1950s weapons have been produced by private companies on a scale previously unimaginable. The idea took hold that in order to intimidate and contain the Soviet Union the U.S. needed to keep its armed forces at something close to a wartime level indefinitely. Today, the prospect of going to war against the Soviet Union around the world appears to be receding.

The Pentagon has very ambitious and expensive military goals. Because of this, there is an inevitable gap between what the military wants to do (or thinks it is required to do) and the resources which are available. . . .

There has been an overemphasis on money as a way to increase military strength. To an alarming degree during the 1980s the U.S. focused on how much money could be spent, not how well it was spent. Attention has been paid to what portion of the Gross National Product (GNP) should be devoted to the military or what the annual percentage increases should be, not whether more money is necessary or would significantly contribute to the nation's security.

The Reagan Administration spent a total of $2.2 trillion dollars on the military. Even taking inflation into account, the 1984 military budget was greater than the 1969 military budget, the peak spending year of the Vietnam War. Never before had the U.S. military budget experienced a 50 percent increase during peacetime. By fanning fears of American military weakness, the Reagan Administration was able to persuade Congress to provide these huge sums of money to the military.

In the 1980s money was spent in haste and without a coherent plan, resulting in inevitable and predictable waste. John Tower, the chairman of the Senate Armed Services Committee in the early 1980s, [stated later,] "I regret my part in front-loading the budget." . . .

Political Spending

Responsibility for decisions to procure unnecessary weapons does not lie only with the military. Another factor is the pressure by contractors who manufacture them and from members of Congress who promote systems built in their districts and states. The motivation of the contractors is easily understood. In many cases the ability of a military contractor to make big profits depends on receiving a contract from the Pentagon. Without one, it may lose money and face financial difficulties.

The Pentagon wants to preserve the vast array of contractors and subcontractors who collectively produce the huge quantities of equipment needed to fight around the world. A contract is often awarded to a particular company to ensure that it stays in business. The awarding of the M-1 tank production contract to the Chrysler Corporation in November 1976 was such a case. This can be expected in a system where the major motivation for building weapons is profit.

Military-Industrial Complex

The top 20 contractors have annual sales to the Pentagon exceeding a billion dollars each and cumulatively capture about 50 percent of the total Pentagon spending on weapons each year. In turn, some of these firms monopolize the production of a specific type of weapon. The percentages of business done by the top four firms are: nuclear submarines (99%), fighter aircraft (97%), attack aircraft (97%), helicopters (93%).

Mike Peters. Reprinted with permission.

Since the Pentagon generally finds the loss of any major contractor unacceptable, due to concern over maintaining an industrial production base for wartime production, contracts are parceled out selectively to firms. Buying weapons primarily to preserve a bloated "defense industrial base" for war with the Soviet Union seems outmoded, particularly as any U.S.-Soviet war would be a short nuclear war.

General Dynamics was awarded the F-111 aircraft contract in 1962 immediately following cancellation of production of its B-58 bomber and was awarded the F-16 in 1974 when F-111 production was ending. McDonnell Douglas was awarded the F-15 fighter aircraft contract in 1970 as the F-4 program was being phased down. Production of the C-5A transport aircraft began at Lockheed as C-141 production ended. For 30 years, Lockheed has provided all of the Navy's submarine ballistic missiles—moving from the Polaris to the Poseidon to the Trident I and now to the Trident II—all on an essentially noncompetitive basis. . . .

Although contractor selection is supposed to be insulated from outside pressures, the pattern of awards has shown a definite tendency to favor firms with political clout. Besides making PAC [political action committee] contributions, firms gain influence by paving honoraria to members of Congress for speeches and by arranging to farm out work to as many subcontractors as possible in key districts and states.

Restoring money for weapons that even the Pentagon does not want is a traditional practice. In 1981 the Defense Department requested no funds for the Cobra/TOW helicopter, but the delegation from Texas where the helicopters were made restored 17 of them to the budget at a cost of $44.5 million. That same year the Administration requested no money for the A-6E attack plane, made by Grumman on Long Island, but the New York delegation saw to it that 12 planes were included in the budget at a cost of $186.7 million. These aircraft were then produced with astonishing inefficiency, the A-6E at the rate of one per month and the Cobra at the rate of 1.5 per month, which pushed costs per weapon to new highs.

In 1989 the Northrop Corporation, with the cooperation of the Pentagon, issued a news release defending the B-2 bomber as a jobs program, stating, "The U.S. Air Force's B-2 program is supported nationwide by tens of thousands of men and women at prime contractor Northrop Corporation, key subcontractors Boeing, LTV, General Electric and Hughes, and other suppliers and subcontractors in 46 states." Buying $600 million aircraft to create jobs is a gross waste of tax dollars. . . .

Illegal Means

Getting a major weapons contract is very profitable and the competition for many contracts is extremely fierce. Thus, at times contractors will resort to illegal means to try to gain an edge in bidding for a contract. This too often results in an unqualified company winning a contract. Consequent delays and attempts to fix problems caused by their own inadequacies increase the price. The trafficking in inside information by defense consultants revealed in the Ill Wind investigation made public in 1988 is a recent example. So far, there have been 2 indictments and 24 guilty pleas from this one investigation. . . .

One of the most serious problems facing the U.S. in attempting to produce useful weapons at reasonable prices is that achievable goals are not set. The problem starts at the very outset of the process, when the military seeks new weapons capable of fighting many kinds of wars all around the world. Congress is not provided the information it needs to judge the need for such weapons. Military contractors make big money by pushing the most expensive, high-tech weapons and aid the military in lobbying Congress to buy new weapons.

This often leads to a process known as "goldplating," the incorporation into a weapon of the newest and most expensive technologies regardless of their battlefield effectiveness or cost. It was this inclination which led to the fiasco of the DIVAD [division air defense gun], a system that was so flawed that former Defense Secretary Caspar Weinberger was forced to cancel its production after an expenditure of $1.8 billion. Norman Augustine, a defense industry official and former Assistant Secretary of the Army, has said, "The last ten percent of performance sought generates one-third of the cost and two-thirds of the problems."

Another weapon which has been afflicted by the "goldplating" syndrome is the Bradley infantry fighting vehicle. The Bradley was to replace the Army's M-113 personnel carrier and was conceived as a motorized infantry combat vehicle which would allow troops to fight while inside. The design kept changing after development began. The TOW [tubular optical guided wire] antitank missile was attached and a complex turret was added. As a result, the weight rose, causing problems with the vehicle's power train and reducing its ability to ford streams. The TOW turret leaves less room for infantrymen, forcing a reduction in squad size to 7 rather than the 9 soldiers judged necessary. The armor is made of aluminum, which is a reactive metal. When it is hit by an antitank round the aluminum vaporizes, becoming chemical fuel for the explosion and intensifying the deadly blast effects.

Understated Costs

When a new weapon finally receives approval from Congress, the promised capabilities for the program are often highly overstated and the costs are greatly understated. This is due in large part to powerful political pressures. Understating costs enables a contractor to submit an artificially low bid in the hope of winning a contract, subsequently making his profits through price increases, spare parts, training programs, and repair programs. The 1986 Reagan-appointed Packard Commission reported that military planners pursue unneeded weapons capabilities. The Commission noted that this tendency "has led to overstated specifications, which have led to higher equipment costs. Such so-called 'goldplating' has become deeply embedded in our system today."

After a design is approved. the next step is allowing firms to compete for contracts for the weapon. Contractors are discouraged from requesting modifications of or pointing out problems with the design. Since a contractor must promise that it will fully satisfy the blueprint, the competition is based mainly on the contractor's optimism. To make a profit, the contractor always remains optimistic. In order to sell their products they often resort to standard marketing techniques: they advertise, they exaggerate, and they criticize their competitors. Yet a low bid is required to win the contract. The usual result is that the company bids low to win the contract and comes back later asking for more.

United Technologies promised to deliver Black Hawk helicopters to the Army for only $2.6 million apiece in the late 1970s, but jacked up the price to $4.7 million each when the deliveries started. Predictably, a major weapon takes too long to produce (10-15 years) and has many cost overruns. . . .

What to Do

The U.S. cannot tolerate a "business-as-usual" approach toward military spending any longer. Changing international conditions, constraints on money, growing technological complexity, and the drive for profits have all combined to produce weapons that are becoming irrelevant to our military needs.

Without appropriate military goals, it is unlikely the Pentagon will buy the weapons truly needed for defending the country. Buying weapons to fight nuclear wars or to defend countries capable of defending themselves does not contribute to the defense of the U.S. . . .

The U.S. would be more likely to buy truly necessary weapons if decisions were not distorted by the desire of contractors to make huge profits from government contracts. To help achieve that, consideration should be given to making it illegal for contractors to contribute money to members of Congress. . . .

In the past decade the Pentagon bought weapons that were not needed because the military and defense contractors had more money than they could spend effectively. In the future it is likely the U.S. will be reducing both its military spending and the size of its armed forces. This will have at least two very positive effects. Smaller military budgets will hopefully restore a sense of discipline in spending taxpayers' dollars. As the U.S. moves to a leaner military force the Pentagon should be able to pay service members more and train them better to operate today's and tomorrow's weapons.

"There is little support in the data for the argument that the defense industry . . . is massively wasteful."

The Defense Industry Is Not Overly Wasteful and Inefficient

Thomas L. McNaugher

While many experts have charged the defense industry with inefficiency and greed, in the following viewpoint Thomas L. McNaugher defends the industry and argues that it is not as inefficient as critics claim. McNaugher states that defending the U.S. is an expensive task, and that if the U.S. wants the best weapons, it must be willing to pay for them. The inefficiencies in defense spending are not the fault of the defense industry, McNaugher concludes, but rather can be blamed on the weapons procurement policies of the Pentagon. McNaugher is a senior fellow in the foreign policy department of the Brookings Institution, a Washington, D.C., think tank.

As you read, consider the following questions:

1. Why does McNaugher believe it is difficult to establish an appropriate cost for U.S. weapons?
2. What does the author conclude from his comparison of U.S. and European weapons?
3. Why does the author think it is unrealistic for the public to expect the defense industry to be perfectly efficient?

Thomas L. McNaugher, *New Weapons, Old Politics: America's Military Procurement Muddle.* Washington, DC: The Brookings Institution, 1989, pp. 1, 166-171, 173-174, 180. Reprinted with permission.

Nobody likes the weapons acquisition process. Vocal critics of American weapons find them overly complex, expensive, and unreliable. Executive and legislative branch officials accuse the firms that produce these weapons of inefficiency, shoddy production practices, even dishonesty—hence the perennial cry of "fraud, waste, and abuse" in the defense sector. Defense industrialists and military procurement managers respond by citing countless congressionally imposed audits that undermine attempts to manage acquisition projects smoothly and efficiently. And almost everyone finds the overall acquisition process, the routines and procedures by which weapons are developed and produced, exasperating in its complexity. It is hard to find a government activity so thoroughly criticized as the way in which the United States develops, produces, fields, and supports weaponry. . . .

Understanding Defense Inefficiencies

The popular perception of waste in the defense industry is based on simple comparisons. In the Reagan era, horror stories about $435 hammers and $640 toilet seats were taken as seemingly irrefutable evidence of waste and inefficiency in the defense industry. Yet the presence of waste in the production of sophisticated weapons is much more difficult to establish than these cases suggest. Efficiency implies a point of reference. A hardware store hammer, for example, tells one that $435 is far too much to pay for a hammer. But what should an F-15 cost—not today, but in 1973, when it first entered the nation's inventory as the world's most advanced fighter aircraft? Ironically, so long as the United States stays technologically ahead of its adversaries (and its allies), U.S. weapons will forever be without firm points of comparison.

Moreover, given its national strategy, the United States should be willing to pay a premium to get the best new technologies to the field quickly; that is what it takes to stay ahead. In this sense, the Soviets, much more than the United States, should be concerned about the efficiency of their defense industry. . . . The United States pays such a premium. There could hardly be a less efficient way to move new weapons to the field than the rush currently imposed on that process. Yet the military routinely justifies this practice as essential to staying ahead, and Congress routinely funds the rush to production, presumably for the same reason. Efficiency, in short, is less important than national security.

In certain cases, efficiency is also less important than domestic politics. For every member of Congress who criticizes waste in the defense industry, there is one who ensures that a defense firm in his or her state or district remains open, even though production rates are inefficiently low. Others hold up production of a new system by forcing the Defense Department to consider yet again a production award fairly granted some years before, thereby forcing taxpayers to carry the cost of an idle production line. Meanwhile, legislation that mandates the allocation of defense procurement funding to small business ensures that production awards will not always be made on the basis of economic or technical merit alone. Here again, commercial comparisons will no doubt surface evidence of waste but not avoidable waste.

A National Asset

The resources that the United States has put together in support of our Armed Forces have been the envy of the world. Without firing a shot, it won what would have been the most destructive war of all time. The infrastructure of scientists, engineers, and manufacturing skills represent an investment of more than $1 trillion. . . . It is a national asset.

Robert B. Costello, *American Legion Magazine,* November 1990.

With commercial comparisons of little use, a better way to get a grip on the question of waste in the defense industry is to compare like commodities. Rough but useful comparisons do exist. For example, one can compare the cost of U.S. weaponry with the cost of comparable European systems, on the assumption that European systems are not likely to be far behind U.S. systems in their degree of technical sophistication. Occasionally production competition is introduced into a U.S. weapons program. Both comparisons offer only ballpark estimates of efficiency and waste. But if the $435 hammer is any indication of the waste found in the defense sector, even ballpark estimates should be useful.

European Comparisons

Finding European points of reference is not as easy as it sounds. The costs of European weapons are difficult to find and interpret. Moreover, because European governments and defense firms depend on weapons exports far more than their U.S. counterparts (since their domestic military markets are much smaller), they tend to hold costs secret, the better to compete in the international market. European production runs are usually smaller than those in the United States, raising overhead costs, and hence average costs, per unit. Finally, fluctuating exchange rates complicate attempts to convert European prices to dollars for purposes of comparison. This makes precise comparisons almost impossible. But rough comparisons do not suggest that massive waste is present in U.S. weapons procurement.

For example, most observers consider West Germany's Leopard II tank and the U.S. Army's M-1 close equivalents in performance. For a brief period in the mid-1970s the U.S. Army considered buying the Leopard II, hence that vehicle's cost became a matter of some concern. Testifying before Congress during this period, the XM-1 program manager noted, "Based upon the best information that we have available from the Germans, the Leopard II today in 1975 dollars would cost a little over $1 million. Our XM-1 cost, in those same 1975 dollars, under the same terms, we estimate to be somewhere between $700,000 and $750,000. Cynics would argue that U.S. Army cost estimates for a tank competing with the Army's XM-1 should not be trusted. Yet the U.S. firm that would have produced the Leopard II on license had it been purchased came to roughly the same conclusion. In a detailed cost analysis, FMC, Inc., determined the Leopard's unit production cost as $520,000 in 1972 dollars, compared with the U.S. Army's XM-1 unit driveaway cost estimate at the time of $507,000 in 1972 dollars. While one might expect the cost estimate of a U.S. firm to include all the waste for which the defense industry is criticized, for this comparison the presence of competition would be expected to control for these extra costs. . . .

Competition Causes Inefficiency

Competition among American defense firms probably does nothing to eliminate the costs of red tape and other accoutrements of the American way of buying weapons. Testifying before the House Industrial Base Panel, for example, one defense subcontractor whose firm did commercial as well as defense business said, "When bidding on government contracts, we factor in the regulatory and administrative requirements, and increase the price quite substantially." The Panel heard from other witnesses that "the price difference for performing Government contracts ranged from 25 percent to double the price charged for comparable commercial contracts." Whether or not competition among American firms encourages efficient production arrangements, it leaves this artificially high base untouched.

Clearly conclusions drawn from studies of competition in defense procurement must be taken with some caution. In their conclusions, IDA analysts argued that "conservative figures for the projection of post competitive savings are 10 percent for split-award buys [in which each firm wins a share of the production run] and 20 percent for winner-take-all buy outs." This suggests that competition can be useful in cutting defense costs. And it suggests that there is some room for savings in the way monopolistic firms operate. But it hardly suggests the kind of massive waste that most critics have in mind when they castigate the defense industry. . . .

Public Perception, Defense Realities

How can one square these arguments with the reality of $435 hammers and $1,000 stool caps? Part of the explanation lies in the practice of buying tools and specialized components in very small quantities, forcing producers to allocate special production costs over a small production run. This hardly accounts for the $1,000 markup on stool caps. Nor does it apply to common items like the hammer. The practice was wasteful, but the source of waste was procedural—the failure to purchase spares in efficiently sized bundles—not waste and abuse in defense firms.

By far the more serious procedural error, however, was ordering parts through the prime contractor for whose system the spare or tool was required. This opened the part's price to three incredibly disproportionate influences. First, labor connected with modifying, packing, or processing the part was paid at wage and benefit levels of skilled aerospace workers. Second, both packing and processing were controlled by military specifications far more stringent than required for most tools and spares. Third, the item was forced to carry part of the prime contractor's overhead. Indeed, even if contractors do not engage in the lateral shift of overloading spare parts to compensate for lower profits elsewhere, overhead loading will add greatly to spare parts costs.

Procedural waste is still waste, and spare parts horror stories prompted the Defense Department to institute reforms designed to "break out" small components, tools, and spare parts, that is, they would be purchased directly by the services, usually under competitive conditions. Yet it remains unclear how much will be saved by reform. Prime contractor overhead will not disappear. It will be reallocated to larger components where it should have been allocated in the first place. Wage rates are not likely to decline in the aerospace industry, nor will workers be laid off because of the absence of still cap production requirements. Meanwhile, Jacques Gansler argues that reform created problems: "Not only did this [the addition of 6,000 people to check the prices of each spare part] shift valuable defense resources from the high-cost items to the low ones, but the added time required . . . doubled the lead time for the military to acquire spare parts. This will mean either spending more money to fill the longer spare parts pipeline or suffering reduced force readiness." The effort to eliminate procedural waste in one area created it in another.

Gansler's argument provides a metaphor for the larger problem of waste in defense procurement. Nothing in the data analyzed suggests that defense firms are losing money. If the game were producing losers, more defense firms would be going out of business. More important, some data support the idea that monopoly production is not entirely efficient. Yet there is little support in the data for the argument that the defense industry alone is massively wasteful. The contracting game can produce $435 hammers, and defense firms can run up standard labor hour costs several times the size of those found in similar private firms. But the excess cost of U.S. weapons in comparison to European weapons, or conversely the savings induced by competition among American defense manufacturers, is often measured in small fractions. This reality may be nothing to be happy about, but it is far from the levels that horror stories often suggest. . . .

No Massive Waste

The industry is not perfectly efficient. But then one should hardly expect it to be. Some of these firms make unique, advanced products whose production eludes common measures of efficiency. The government often purchases quantities so small that monopoly is the only reasonable means of production. This sector is so far from the free market of economic theory that even the effort to impose competition on defense procurement seems artificial, however useful in specific cases. If comparisons are made to similar items rather than to the private sector, there is little suggestion of massive waste in production.

Distinguishing Between Fact and Opinion

This activity is designed to help develop the basic reading and thinking skill of distinguishing between fact and opinion. Consider the following statement as an example: "The Bush administration proposed spending $307 billion for military purposes in fiscal year 1991." This is a factual statement because it could be verified by checking government reports on the federal budget. But the statement "There is simply no rationale for a defense budget of the size contemplated by the Bush administration" is an opinion. It is debatable whether $307 billion is too much to spend on defense.

When investigating controversial issues it is important that one be able to distinguish between statements of fact and statements of opinion. It is also important to recognize that not all statements of fact are true. They may appear to be true, but some are based on inaccurate or false information. For this activity, however, we are concerned with understanding the difference between those statements which appear to be factual and those which appear to be based primarily on opinion.

Most of the following statements are taken from the viewpoints in this chapter. Consider each statement carefully. *Mark O for any statement you believe is an opinion or interpretation of facts. Mark F for any statement you believe is a fact. Mark I for any statement you believe is impossible to judge.*

If you are doing this activity as a member of a class or group, compare your answers with those of other class or group members. Be able to defend your answers. You may discover that others come to different conclusions than you do. Listening to the reasons others present for their answers may give you valuable insights into distinguishing between fact and opinion.

O = opinion
F = fact
I = impossible to judge

134

1. Mikhail Gorbachev has already made unilateral cuts in Soviet conventional forces.

2. Many European nations have now come close to, and in some cases have surpassed, America's levels of per capita wealth and income.

3. The U.S. cannot tolerate a "business-as-usual" approach to military spending any longer.

4. In the future it is likely the U.S. will be reducing both its military spending and the size of its armed forces.

5. Most media coverage of defense issues accepts without question the premises put forward by the defense establishment.

6. America's largest one-year post-Vietnam cut in defense was 0.9 percent of the gross national product.

7. The federal government has the responsibility to spend whatever is needed to ensure our national security.

8. The United States should be willing to pay a premium to get the best new technologies to the field quickly.

9. One bomb on a B-52 costs $11,000—enough money to run a medical clinic in Bangladesh for one month.

10. Investing the peace dividend in U.S. social programs is the best way to strengthen America's economy.

11. Western economies have thrived in comparison to Eastern-bloc economies.

12. In 1987, there were 61,000 business failures in the United States.

13. Soviet military power is growing even as the Warsaw Pact disintegrates.

14. While the U.S. invests bout 6 percent of its gross national product on defense, the Soviets spend 25 percent or more.

15. The top twenty defense contractors have annual sales to the Pentagon exceeding a billion dollars each.

16. The United States should not reduce its strategic arsenal without corresponding reductions on the Soviet side.

17. The defense budget could be cut in half over the next ten years and the United States and its allies would still be secure.

18. More and more, the U.S. is buying weapons it does not need and is spending too much for the weapons it does buy.

Periodical Bibliography

The following articles have been selected to supplement the diverse views presented in this chapter.

John Barry — "The Coming Cutbacks in Military Money," *Newsweek*, March 18, 1991.

Gary S. Becker — "Defense Spending Isn't Stunting the U.S. Economy," *Business Week*, February 25, 1991.

Robert Borosage — "How Bush Kept the Guns from Turning into Butter," *Rolling Stone*, February 21, 1991.

Center for Defense Information — "A New Military Budget for a New World," *The Defense Monitor*, vol. 20, no. 2, 1991. Available from the Center for Defense Information, 1500 Massachusetts Ave. NW, Washington, DC 20005.

Eliot A. Cohen — "Check, Please," *The New Republic*, April 1, 1991.

Anthony Cordesman — "America's New Combat Culture," *The New York Times*, February 28, 1991.

Erik Eckholm — "In Detente and Cutbacks Navy Has Powerful Foes," *The New York Times*, May 22, 1990.

William Greider — "Protecting the Pentagon," *Utne Reader*, March/April 1991.

William R. Hawkins — "New Enemies for Old?" *National Review*, September 17, 1990.

Elizabeth Kimbrough — "Is Economic Conversion the Answer?" *Forward Motion*, August 1990. Available from PO Box 1884, Jamaica Plain, MA 02130.

Daniel Maguire — "Demilitarizing Our Budget Dollars," *Christianity Today*, March 5, 1990.

Richard Perle — "Watching Over Defense," *The American Enterprise*, May/June 1990.

Nancy J. Perry — "More Spinoffs from Defense," *Fortune*, special issue, Spring/Summer 1991.

Jonathan Schlefer — "Defense Against What?" *Technology Review*, January 1991.

Timothy W. Stanley — "Defense: The Pentagon's Perestroika," *The American Legion Magazine*, June 1990.

What Weapons Would Strengthen America's Defense?

AMERICA'S DEFENSE

Chapter Preface

During the 1980s, the U.S. spent billions of dollars building up an arsenal of high-technology weapons. Critics argued that it was unwise to spend vast amounts of money on weapons that had not been tried in actual combat. However, the 1991 Persian Gulf War demonstrated that many of these advanced weapons functioned exceptionally well. In the Gulf, the U.S. and its allies shot down Iraqi Scud missiles with Patriot missiles, bombed Baghdad with Tomahawk cruise missiles launched from warships hundreds of miles away, and used other high-tech weapons effectively. Many military officials claimed that U.S. superior technology was a major factor in defeating Iraq quickly and decisively.

Defense experts who believe the success in Iraq proves the worthiness of advanced weapons are now encouraging the Pentagon to increase its investment in such weapons. Heritage Foundation policy analyst Baker Spring supports investing in advanced weapons and argues that, although they are expensive, they are worth the cost. "Technology is the 'force multiplier' that allows U.S. forces to shoot farther and more precisely than their enemies. The best is always expensive, but the price for deploying anything less ultimately will be paid in the lives of American soldiers, sailors, and airmen," Spring concludes.

Yet many Americans balk at spending tax dollars on high-priced weapons. One Patriot missile, for example, costs approximately $1.4 million. In addition, some experts doubt that advanced weapons will significantly improve America's defense. They argue that while advanced weapons did prove to be reliable in the Persian Gulf War, the professionalism of the soldiers, the success of traditional weapons, and the condition and morale of the Iraqi troops were just as vital in ensuring victory. Massachusetts Democratic representative Barney Frank supports this assertion, stating that advanced weapons "were irrelevant to victory in Iraq and will be to future conflicts of this sort." Critics also charge that while the deserts of the Middle East proved ideal for laser-guided, high-tech weapons, such weapons may be of little use in jungle warfare such as that experienced in Vietnam.

The question of what weapons will best protect the U.S. is an issue of both defense and expense. The following chapter presents arguments concerning which weapons the U.S. should purchase, which it can afford to purchase, and which will offer the best protection for the nation.

"Over the next decade the United States will continue to require capable, credible conventional forces."

The U.S. Must Maintain Its Conventional Arsenal

Carl E. Vuono

With the improved relations between the U.S. and the Soviet Union, some experts argue that the U.S. should reduce the size of its conventional arsenal. In the following viewpoint, Carl E. Vuono disagrees with this proposition. Vuono argues that only a strong conventional military can protect the U.S. and its allies from the threat posed by turmoil in Eastern Europe and the Third World. Conventional weapons are the foundation of America's defense, the author believes, and are the only practical and effective way to deter aggression from leaders such as Saddam Hussein. Vuono, a general in the U.S. military, has been Chief of Staff of the U.S. Army since 1987.

As you read, consider the following questions:

1. What example does the author give to show that military power is still important in the world?
2. Why does Vuono believe it would be dangerous for the U.S. to ignore the Third World?
3. How did the Persian Gulf War reveal the importance of conventional weapons, in the author's opinion?

Carl E. Vuono, "Desert Storm and the Future of Conventional Forces," *Foreign Affairs,* Spring 1991. Reprinted by permission of *Foreign Affairs.* Copyright © 1991 by the Council on Foreign Relations, Inc.

In the coming decades the United States confronts not only a revolution in international affairs but urgent calls to adapt its military strategy and forces. Some commentators go so far as to assert that the world is on the threshold of a new era in which military power will no longer be of central importance. Others recognize future challenges but argue that the United States can no longer shoulder the burden of military leadership in a time of enormous budget deficits at home and increasing economic competition abroad. Still others assert that America neither needs nor can afford the range of forces it maintained during the Cold War.

A Dangerous International Environment

These perspectives, however, are dangerously shortsighted. While the risk of a major conflict with the Soviet Union has certainly ebbed to a 45-year low, Iraq's aggression against Kuwait clearly demonstrates that the international environment remains dangerous and is in many respects growing more complex. U.S. interests around the globe have inextricably entangled this nation in world affairs. If the United States is to protect these interests and ensure its security in the post-Cold War world, it must maintain military forces capable of meeting a full array of contingencies. Over the next decade the United States will continue to require capable, credible conventional forces as the central element of its national military strategy.

In an era of decreasing resources devoted to defense, the critical issue is how to properly shape U.S. conventional forces. Adjustment need not imply a wholesale restructuring of forces or doctrines. As we have seen during Operation Desert Storm in the Persian Gulf, many elements of military strategy and force design that served the nation so well throughout the Cold War will remain relevant in the era that follows. . . .

Military Power Is Still Important

The international security environment is undergoing significant and, in some areas, revolutionary change. Military power nonetheless remains a dominant feature of relations between states. It is instructive to remember that Saddam Hussein imposed his will on Kuwait and threatened to alter the international economic order with Iraqi divisions, not dollars. And it was with military power that the international community ultimately redressed Iraq's aggression in Operation Desert Storm. It should be apparent from this experience alone that it is premature for the United States to abandon strong military forces.

The design of U.S. forces, however, requires a clear assessment of the military challenges the nation will face. Perhaps the most difficult challenge to frame is that which will emerge from the Soviet Union. Despite better relations with the United States and unprecedented U.S.-Soviet cooperation during the early stages of the crisis in the gulf, future Soviet policy remains uncertain. The enduring strength of the Soviet military must remain an important factor in determining the size and shape of U.S. forces. . . .

Regional Crises Pose Threat to Peace

Regional crises will not end and the United States as a global superpower will be expected to play a role in conflict resolution. Rising nationalism, ethnic and religious strife, missile proliferation and America's dependence on foreign energy sources all confirm the necessity to retain conventional military capabilities to intervene rapidly and effectively when the security interests of the United States and our allies are at stake.

Don Snider and Jeff Shaffer, *The Washington Times*, June 12, 1990.

The historic changes now underway in the Soviet Union and eastern Europe could lead to instability and conflict. There certainly are reasons to hope that relaxation of East-West tensions will usher in a new era of peace and general prosperity in Europe. But recent events in the Soviet Union and eastern Europe demonstrate the potential for violence as the collapsing Soviet empire struggles with cataclysmic change. Unrest may stem from unfulfilled expectations and nationalist animosities, heretofore held in check by communism and the East-West rivalry. Such unrest could ignite armed conflict within and among European nations and directly jeopardize U.S. or allied interests, or invite Soviet intervention.

The threat posed by instability in Europe defies empirical evaluation. There are no quantitative indices—numbers of tanks or aircraft—against which one can measure U.S. requirements. Genuine dangers may nonetheless emerge from a Europe adrift in change. Accordingly, Washington must build its post-containment commitment to Europe with an eye to history and with the conviction that the United States can make a lasting contribution to stabilizing the continent.

Challenges in the developing world are serious as well. The military power wielded by developing nations is no longer insignificant, as the Iraqi arsenal forcefully demonstrated. Rivalries among nations, religious and ideological hatreds, and ambitions for economic and political power remain. These sources of instability are made more dangerous by the proliferation of sophisticated weapons—from modern armor to ballistic missiles —that can produce violence of unprecedented magnitude.

141

Tank battles in the 1967 and 1973 Arab-Israeli wars, for example, resulted in levels of destruction rivaling those projected for a superpower conflict on the plains of Europe. These were hardly isolated cases; the Iran-Iraq war of the 1980s was characterized by tank engagements, intense artillery duels, ballistic missile exchanges and chemical attacks, and the toll in human life numbered more than one million. Allied forces in Saudi Arabia confronted an Iraq armed with hundreds of Scud missiles and more than 5,000 tanks, a formidable conventional force by any standard. Indeed, the final defeat of the Republican Guard required the coalition to amass and employ the largest tank formations since World War II.

Nor do the nations of the Middle East and Persian Gulf have a monopoly on strong military forces. A growing number of countries now have the ability to engage in sustained, mechanized land combat. The armies of Vietnam and North Korea, for example, are among the largest in the world. A dozen nations in the developing world have more than 1,000 tanks in their land forces. Ballistic and cruise missiles are spreading to many parts of the world. Chemical weapons are also entering the inventories of a growing list of nations, and the proliferation of nuclear capabilities continues to present an ominous threat.

To be sure, aggregate numbers of weapons in the developing world do not in themselves reflect the degree of threat these nations pose. The danger in the proliferation of weapons lies not in the numbers themselves, but in the capabilities those weapons give regimes with whom the United States and its allies and friends have conflicting interests. A number of such regimes exist, and as much as some might wish to ignore these trends in the developing world, they command the attention of the United States.

Low-Intensity Conflict

There is, finally, the ongoing problem of low-intensity conflict in the developing world, manifest in insurgencies, international terrorism and illicit drug trafficking. Low-intensity conflicts generally cannot be resolved through the application of military power alone; they require the integrated application of political, economic and military measures to address the causes as well as the manifestations of unrest. The importance of properly trained, structured and equipped armed forces is nevertheless a critical element of a comprehensive strategy to address these types of conflicts. Low-intensity conflict will remain in the coming years a significant challenge for the U.S. military.

The United States clearly need not, and indeed should not, insert itself in every regional squabble. But it does not have the luxury of treating warfare in the developing world with indifference. The archaic concept of "fortress America" simply retains no strategic relevance for the United States in the 1990s. Military strategists and political leaders must anticipate that U.S. forces will be called on to advance and protect American interests in regional conflicts ranging from insurgencies to full-scale conventional wars against powerful land armies. U.S. forces must be capable of meeting those challenges.

Gauging the Threat

Now that we see the military power of the Warsaw Pact disintegrating, there will be those who argue that the Soviet empire never amounted to much, that Western estimates of the strength of the Warsaw Pact were deliberately exaggerated with a view to inflating the U.S. defense budget. Only now, we will hear it argued, has the world come to accept what the left has been preaching throughout the Cold War: that the Soviets and their East European military chattels were not to be feared.

This is of more than passing historical interest. For it will be necessary for some time to come to gauge correctly the threat still posed by Soviet military power in judging how to protect our security and how to shape our military budget. As we seek wise counsel, we should be wary of accepting the weight and authority of those who never acknowledged Soviet power when it was growing and who now ignore how much of it remains. So before running to the bank with the elusive "peace dividend," it would be wise to remember that Soviet military power remains formidable and that it is growing even as the Warsaw Pact disintegrates.

Richard Perle, *The American Enterprise*, May/June 1990.

Conventional forces provide the United States with unique capabilities across an expanding range of military requirements—from peacetime engagement, through deterrence, to the conduct of major war.

In peacetime, conventional forces are the bedrock of America's military-to-military contacts with the forces of over 130 other nations. The United States provides military training, in one form or another, to 75 percent of the world's armed forces. This training is crucial to the successful assimilation of new weapons and tactics by friendly forces. More important, U.S. military training is a unique medium for encouraging the adoption of the values of professionalism, respect for human rights and support for democratic institutions. U.S. conventional forces provide an indispensable avenue of influence and a source of positive change in many nations where political and social traditions accord the military a prominent role in the government. Conventional forces, particularly the U.S. Army, actively support nation-building in countries throughout the world, assisting in the development of infrastructure that, in turn, helps alleviate some of the root causes of instability and violence.

Fighting Drug Trafficking

Conventional forces also make an important contribution to the national counternarcotics strategy. As one element of a comprehensive approach, military units are helping law enforcement agencies detect and defeat drug trafficking. Mobile U.S. training teams advise the security forces of drug producing countries, and conventional forces provide equipment, maintenance support and training to U.S. government agencies that fight trafficking, both in the United States and abroad.

Conventional forces are also among the most effective tools for enhancing political stability in the international order. U.S. ground forces in Korea and elsewhere in East Asia have provided security, and thus encouraged ancient enemies—for example, Japan, Korea and China—to manage their differences without resorting to force. Without American willingness to sustain peacekeeping forces in the Sinai, the historic peace treaty between Israel and Egypt might never have materialized.

Perhaps nowhere is the stabilizing role of U.S. conventional forces more evident than in Europe. NATO [North Atlantic Treaty Organization], the most successful and enduring alliance in recent memory, created and sustained an environment of military and political cooperation among nations whose histories gave them every reason to be as suspicious of one another as they were of the Soviets. The United States contributed to the unparalleled success of the alliance by providing leadership unencumbered by the historical baggage of regional animosities or territorial ambitions.

Closely related to their role in enhancing political stability, conventional forces are equally crucial to deterring aggression in places where the United States has a sizable military presence and in other regions where it has no forward-deployed forces. Each element of conventional forces contributes substantially to deterrence. Naval forces, including Marine Corps elements, can quickly project military power in order to demonstrate U.S. concern; air power, particularly when surged into a crisis area, can rapidly bolster the credibility of U.S. involvement and increase the ability to punish aggression. Historically there has been no stronger statement of national resolve than the deployment of the American soldier. The presence of U.S. Army units on the ground—combat elements that cannot sail or fly away overnight—leaves little doubt that the full power and prestige of the United States are committed.

Finally, conventional forces have the responsibility to fight and win wars. They have the combat power necessary to determine the outcome of battle and to preserve American interests, should deterrence fail. The key to the successful employment of conventional combat power in war is to fight jointly—a lesson that stood in stark relief in Desert Storm. In only the rarest of circumstances can either sea, land or air power be effective by itself. Joint operations do not require that each element of conventional forces commit equal numbers of troops or equipment; there is no scientific formula for the proportions needed from each service. Rather, in joint operations each service contributes its unique capabilities to the mission at hand. That is the way U.S. forces fought in Iraq and Kuwait, and that is how they must fight in the future. Indeed, it is no exaggeration to assert that U.S. conventional forces will fight jointly, or they will not fight at all. . . .

The Persian Gulf War

Perhaps the most persuasive demonstration of the importance of conventional forces is the American reaction to Iraq's seizure of Kuwait. Without attempting to reconstruct a comprehensive history of the crisis, it is apparent that the versatility, deployability, lethality and expansibility of American conventional forces were the keys to the U.S. response to Saddam Hussein's aggression. . . .

Desert Storm began with operations designed to neutralize the most dangerous Iraqi offensive and defensive capabilities, to diminish Iraq's ability to sustain its forces occupying Kuwait and to directly attack the combat capabilities of Iraq's land forces. Once these objectives were achieved, the final phase began. The last phase had two basic objectives: to drive Iraqi forces from Kuwait and to deny to Saddam Hussein the ability to reinforce the theater or to pose a threat to Kuwait in the future. This second objective required the defeat of the Republican Guard divisions based in southern Iraq—divisions that were indeed Saddam Hussein's strategic center of gravity and the source of his regional power.

The successful conduct of the final phase of Operation Desert Storm was a powerful demonstration of the effectiveness of conventional forces operating jointly to achieve objectives attainable in no other way. The plan envisioned a deliberate attack into Kuwait, to fix Iraqi forces in place, while two U.S. Army corps swept around to the west of Iraqi defenses in an audacious turning movement designed to envelop and destroy the Republican Guard. Air support was a fundamental dimension of this plan, which pitted allied maneuverability against static Iraqi defenses, to terminate the war with as few U.S. and coalition casualties as possible. Seldom in organized warfare has a plan been so flawlessly executed. . . .

At the most basic level, the coalition prevented Iraq from executing its style of war. It isolated Iraqi forces from their support base, weakened them by continuous bombardment, successfully disguised the time and place of the thrust of the coalition's attack and defeated the Republican Guard. Although much more remains to be done to translate military success into political stability, the United States and the international coalition clearly won a victory of almost unprecedented dimensions. And, in the final analysis, it was a victory that rested on the capability of U.S. conventional forces.

The Iraqi invasion of Kuwait and the international counteroffensive that ultimately defeated that aggression thus underscore the future role of conventional forces. Saddam Hussein persuasively demonstrated that smaller nations in the developing world can indeed affect the international community in a profound way. He showed that such states have the capacity to conduct high-intensity conflict and to attack with little or no warning. Moreover, he demonstrated a troubling feature of international relations today: many regimes still operate from a frame of reference in which the force of arms remains a legitimate—and too often preferred—form of international discourse. If nothing else is learned from Desert Storm, it is that the sun has not set on violence and warfare, and that the conventional forces of this nation remain an indispensable element in the quiver of American power.

A World of Challenges

As the United States confronts a truly revolutionary era, the nation must have the courage to see the world as it really is: a world abundant with opportunities, but also one beset by challenges; a world in which conflict remains a way of life for many nations; and a world in which the interests of the United States remain very much at risk. In this world, military strategy must be built on the continued primacy of conventional forces—supported by a sufficient nuclear arsenal—essential to the preservation of peace and to the shaping of a future in which freedom and democracy are allowed to prosper. The nation must shape its forces to meet the challenges of a new era. The American people and the world expect, and deserve, nothing less.

"The conventional defense of Western Europe now costs the United States about $126 billion a year, of which no more than $22 billion has to do with maintaining a significant U.S. presence in Europe."

The Conventional Arsenal Can Be Decreased

William W. Kaufmann

The United States can and should reduce the size of its conventional weaponry, William W. Kaufmann contends in the following viewpoint. Kaufmann argues that a large arsenal of conventional weapons is expensive and unnecessary, especially now that Mikhail Gorbachev has drastically cut Soviet conventional forces. The author believes that reducing conventional forces will not endanger America's security and will strengthen U.S.-Soviet relations. Kaufmann is a scholar at the Brookings Institution, a Washington, D.C., think tank.

As you read, consider the following questions:

1. Why did U.S. defense spending increase so dramatically from 1980 to 1990, according to the author?
2. For what two reasons has the Pentagon supported America's large amount of conventional weapons, in Kaufmann's opinion?
3. Why does the author oppose introducing new conventional weapons?

Excerpted, with permission, from *Glasnost, Perestroika, and U.S. Defense Spending* by William W. Kaufmann. Washington, DC: The Brookings Institution, 1990, pp. 1-4, 21-25, 46-47.

147

Mikhail S. Gorbachev's rise to the summit of the Soviet government and the changes he has instituted in the communist bloc and international relations since 1986 raise an urgent question. To what extent should the United States alter its defense establishment, programs, and budgets during the last decade of the twentieth century? The Bush administration proposed to spend nearly $300 billion on national defense in fiscal 1990, and both the executive branch and a majority of Congress seemed to take that amount as a fact of life and as appropriate to existing international conditions. From a somewhat different perspective, however, such a commitment of national resources might be seen as the abnormal result of some quite abnormal circumstances that, if altered, would produce substantial reductions in defense spending.

Trends in U.S. Defense Spending

After all, it was only a little more than fifty years ago that U.S. defense spending amounted to $14 billion (in 1990 dollars) and took less than 2 percent of the nation's gross national product. Even in the wake of World War II, with all the new international responsibilities thrust upon the United States, national defense spending between 1947 and 1950 averaged approximately $101 billion a year, admittedly influenced in part by the American monopoly of atomic weapons. Only after the U.S. vision of a cooperative world order under the aegis of the United Nations fell victim to Stalin's subjugation of Eastern Europe, his attempts to subvert the democracies of Western Europe, the Soviet blockade of West Berlin, the seizure of power in China by Mao Tse-tung, and the outbreak of the Korean War did American policy shift fully from cooperation to containment. By 1949 the United States had become a founding member of the North Atlantic Treaty Organization (NATO). The war in Korea hardened the American view of the Soviet Union as an expansionist power, led to a rapid growth in U.S. security commitments to Asia, and began an era of large increases in the defense budget.

The growth in spending was uneven. President Dwight D. Eisenhower tried to bring the defense budget down after the truce in Korea, but it still remained more than twice as high as it had been before the war, in large part because of the expansion of U.S. nuclear capabilities. After further increases and decreases under presidents Kennedy, Johnson, Nixon, Ford, and Carter, President Ronald Reagan gave an upward impetus to defense spending that was unprecedented in American peacetime history. Between 1980 and 1990, outlays for national defense grew in real terms by nearly 35 percent. Between 1950 (before the North Korean attack) and 1990, those same outlays expanded by a factor of nearly three—from approximately $106 billion to $300 billion—even as they declined as a percent of a growing GNP [gross national product].

No Need for U.S. Forces

The continued presence of U.S. conventional forces in Europe is unwarranted. . . .

The termination of our commitment to NATO would eliminate the need for a substantial portion of U.S. forces. More than 320,000 personnel are currently stationed in Europe. . . .

The removal and demobilization of those forces would save approximately $50 billion per year. But that is not the extent of the potential savings. An additional 6 Army divisions and 37 tactical air squadrons stationed in the United States are earmarked for the reinforcement of Western Europe within 10 days of mobilization. Moreover, a sizable portion of the Navy's Second Fleet stationed in the Atlantic (typically 6 aircraft carrier battle groups, 1 or 2 battleship surface attack groups, and other units) as well as America's air- and sealift capacity exist because of the European mission. Eliminating those "reserve" elements plus the forces actually stationed in the European theater would enable the United States to save $110 billion to $115 billion of the $130 billion now being spent annually on NATO.

Ted Galen Carpenter and Rosemary Fiscarelli, *A Cato Institute White Paper: America's Peace Dividend,* August 7, 1990.

The trend in Soviet defense expenditures is much more difficult not only to ascertain but also to equate in comparable terms with what has happened in the United States. However, use of the dollar-costing methodology of the CIA [Central Intelligence Agency] (which calculates the price of buying the Soviet military establishment in the U.S. economy) suggests that the two countries started from about the same spending base after World War II. During the 1950s and 1960s, however, the United States appears to have outspent the Soviet Union, largely because of the defense cutbacks made by General Secretary Nikita S. Khrushchev. With the advent of Leonid I. Brezhnev, this policy was reversed, and Soviet outlays began to average an annual real growth of approximately 3 percent until the mid-1970s. Since then, real growth has been 2 percent or less a year and, according to Gorbachev, has not grown at all since 1987. Nonetheless, it would appear that the two countries were on about equal terms in defense spending by the end of the 1980s, although defense as a share of the Soviet GNP was probably at least three times higher than the comparable share of defense in the United States. In other words, if both sides roughly tripled their defense spending during the last forty years, the burden fell much more painfully on the Soviet Union than on the United States in its consumption of resources in general and modern technology in particular.

The Current Situation

Despite these expenditures—or perhaps because of them—the two principal spheres of influence (with one major exception) remained remarkably stable regardless of frequent forecasts of an imminent Soviet breakout in Europe, Africa, the Middle East, Southwest Asia, and even Latin America. The one great exception, of course, was the departure of China, not from communist dictatorship but from the communist bloc. Elsewhere, whatever changes occurred, their significance proved more symbolic than substantive.

Whether Khrushchev, had he remained in power, would or could have ended the military competition and removed its underlying causes remains uncertain. What does seem clear is that Gorbachev is moving well beyond what Khrushchev had begun to attempt. At a minimum, Gorbachev appears to be looking for a long respite from the cold war. More optimistically (and quite conceivably), he is seeking, among other goals, to reform the political and economic systems of the Soviet Union, to end the cold war and the military competition, and to shift resources from the military sector to the civilian economy. As evidence of his sincerity, he has withdrawn Soviet forces from Afghanistan and encouraged settlement of the conflicts in Namibia, Angola, and Cambodia. . . . Somewhat to the consternation of the industrial democracies he has asked to become included in their deliberations.

Gorbachev's Long-Term Motives

Equally important, Gorbachev has tried through both unilateral and collaborative measures to emphasize that the Soviet Union is more interested in military stability between the major alliances at reduced cost than in military advantages, offensive action and preemption, and a heavy-handed control over countries bordering on the Soviet Union. . . .

He has announced a cut of 500,000 in the Soviet armed forces and agreed to the establishment of conventional parity between NATO and the Warsaw Pact in the area of the Atlantic to the Urals, even though, once again, that will require the Pact to give up more personnel and weapons than NATO. Beyond all that, Gorbachev has announced that Soviet military doctrine would be reoriented toward defensive operations, told the East European nations to choose their own paths to socialism, and seem-

150

ingly repudiated the Brezhnev doctrine, which declared the right of the Soviet Union to intervene militarily to uphold communist rule in Eastern Europe.

One can certainly argue about Gorbachev's long-term motives in unleashing this torrent of proposals, actions, and reactions. One can also insist that the Soviet Union show greater movement toward human rights and democracy before the United States and its allies engage in far-reaching modifications of their current military capabilities. But it is worth remembering as well that Gorbachev seems to be offering a respite from the cold war that could last at least a generation and that the United States also has incentives to reduce the military confrontation and competition even if they should resume at a later date. It is not as if America lacked economic problems of its own, although there are many ways to solve them without any changes in programmed defense spending. Nonetheless, reductions in defense—if justifiable on military grounds—would offer some help in meeting a number of social and economic demands, however unlikely it is that feasible reductions would make all problems disappear. . . .

The conventional forces of the United States represent a . . . high order of cost. When investment, operations, and direct and indirect support are charged to these forces, they comprise 80 percent or more of defense outlays. For nearly thirty years the Pentagon has justified such a large effort on two grounds: first, that it would raise the nuclear threshold, and second, that it was the price of having to support allies in Europe and Asia against simultaneous attacks launched by the Soviet Union and its allies with little or no warning. Thus arose what became known in the 1960s as the 2½ and thereafter (with the change in Chinese policy) as the 1½ war strategy.

These descriptions have oversimplified both the apparent objectives of the Joint Chiefs of Staff and the demands that would be made on U.S. conventional forces in a major emergency. Should a war-threatening crisis arise in Europe, for example, U.S. ground and tactical air forces would attempt to deploy, or reinforce deployed forces (as in Germany and Korea), in seven different theaters with a total of thirty-two division forces and forty-one fighter-attack wings drawn from the active and reserve Army, Marine Corps, and Air Force. Efforts to mobilize large quantities of airlift and sealift would be made to ensure the timely deployment of the fighting units. In addition, the Navy would be called upon to help control the major sea lines of communications to Europe, the Mediterranean, Northeast Asia, and the Persian Gulf and would probably seek to launch several power projection operations with its carrier battle groups and Marine amphibious forces in areas such as North Norway and Thrace.

A Holding Action

Whatever one may think of this strategy—which, at least initially, would constitute a holding action—current U.S. capabilities, practically speaking, are not sufficient to meet these multiple and more or less simultaneous demands. The strategy depends on high readiness and rapid response not only in the active-duty but also in the large reserve forces now maintained by the United States. Yet, though current ground and tactical air forces are nearly adequate in force size and composition for their missions, their reserve components (in the National Guard and Reserve), on which they have come to depend so heavily, could probably not meet the standards of readiness and deployability that the strategy seems to require. Equally troublesome, especially given the very conservative assumption that the USSR would attack in several theaters at once and that cohorts such as North Korea and Cuba would join in the fray—all after only a few days of usable warning—airlift and sealift would be in short supply, despite the efforts of the Air Force to obtain 66 million ton-miles of airlift a day, an increase in the Navy's sealift, and the pre-positioning of heavy equipment and supplies both on land and at sea in Europe, the Indian Ocean, and Northeast Asia. To make matters worse, the Navy—because of its emphasis on carrier battle groups, power projections, and amphibious operations—would probably have more carrier battle groups on hand than it would know what to do with and too few escorts and mine warfare ships for the less glamorous but more critical tasks of protecting convoys of reinforcement and supplies needed to sustain forces in widely dispersed theaters. But even supposing that all these proposed deployments could take place, that forward defenses could be established in the key theaters, and that the principal sea-lanes could be adequately protected, there would probably be a shortage of the war reserve stocks needed to sustain overseas operations long enough to permit adequate support from existing or expanded production lines in the United States, especially if simultaneous conflicts were in progress. . . .

Taking Moscow Seriously

A way to deal with the problem would take Soviet arms reductions with the utmost seriousness and have the Pentagon make reciprocal moves of its own. If such an approach appears to surrender too many bargaining chips or to jeopardize U.S. security, it is worth recalling what Gorbachev is already doing without any bargaining at all. He is reducing Soviet ground and tactical air forces by 500,000 men, taking out from East Germany, Czechoslovakia, and Hungary 50,000 of this total and 6 tank divisions. He is also pushing the Soviet military to adopt a doctrine of "nonoffensive defense" to replace the current strategy of preemptive conventional attack into Western Europe or, failing that, "a counter offensive with overwhelming artillery and mechanized forces." Perhaps of greater interest, he and his prime minister, Nikolai I. Ryzhkov, have begun to talk more specifically about the Soviet defense budget and how they propose to cut it. Although the figures used by the two men do not quite agree, Gorbachev maintains that defense spending has not increased since 1987 and that he plans to reduce it by 14.2 percent. Ryzhkov goes even further and talks of cutting defense spending by a third to a half. All these steps are worth encouraging, not by increasing U.S. defense spending and the modernization of its forces, but by relaxing to some degree that U.S. effort. To go further, the opportunity now exists to reconcile U.S. strategy with U.S. forces and budgets.

At this point there is no need, with certain exceptions, to drop any of the contingencies for which the Pentagon has been planning. Instead, in this period of transition, it seems reasonable to assume much less simultaneity in their occurrence—perhaps only one at a time—and much more time in which to prepare for any large attack. At present, for example, defense planners assume that, at best, they will have ten days of usable warning before a major Pact assault on Western Europe. That, in turn, means a heavy dependence on pre-positioned equipment, airlift, and metronomic precision in force deployments, and it demands high readiness in both active and reserve forces. However, as the Soviets withdraw crack divisions from Eastern Europe, while East Germany, Czechoslovakia, Bulgaria, Poland, and Hungary announce reductions in their conventional forces, the probability of a large, short-warning attack declines appreciably. Instead of ten days, something on the order of ninety days of usable warning seems plausible. That means more of an opportunity to bring reserve forces up to active standards of readiness, to discontinue efforts to expand pre-positioning and airlift, and to place greater reliance on sealift. Indeed, in light of the weapons-counting rules under consideration at the CFE [Conventional Forces in Europe] negotiations in Vienna, where the Soviets insist that U.S. pre-positioned equipment be included in the totals, it might make sense to return some of that equipment to the United States and give it to the National Guard and Reserve rather than fund additional weapons for those forces. . . .

No New Weapons Needed

There are also several grounds for questioning the need to introduce a new generation of costly conventional weapons at this time. Ordinarily, defense rolls over its inventory of weapons, on the average, every twenty years and spends a great deal of money upgrading the existing inventory in between. Now, however, the services—without yet having completed the acquisition of the generation of weapons introduced in the mid-1970s—is attempting to field follow-on capabilities that will be even more expensive in real terms to buy, operate, and maintain. Besides, these new weapons, many of which are undergoing concurrent test, evaluation, and production, are designed to deal with threats that may well vanish under the pressure of massive Soviet deficits, defense budget cuts, and the reductions in arms that Gorbachev so badly needs. . . .

Several key points are in need of greater recognition than they have received so far. First, a revolution in military affairs could be in the making at least in part because of the economic distress in the USSR and the changes in Soviet leadership. Granted the revolution may not go as far as has been suggested here. But one thing is clear: the revolution will not progress much further without initiatives from and cooperation by the United States. Second, caution may be in order for Washington, but not to the point of refusing to think about what would constitute a plausibly desirable future in the military realm, how we might get there, and what difference it would make to the defense establishment, defense industry, and research and development. Third, whatever else the United States may decide to do in aid of Gorbachev, it can collaborate with him to reallocate resources from the defense to the civil sector. That will probably help him more than any economic assistance the United States could or would provide. And, as Secretary of State James A. Baker III has pointed out, agreements on arms reductions could have a longer-term effect even if Gorbachev fell from office.

Admittedly, the path projected here could have many twists and turns, and the end does not promise all sweetness and light. Canada, West Germany, France, Italy, Japan, the United Kingdom, and the United States are already making efforts to prevent the proliferation of missiles and chemical weapons as well as nuclear weapons. But potential belligerents such as North and South Korea, India and Pakistan, Iran and Iraq, Syria and Israel—among others—continue to maintain or seek to acquire these capabilities. Regional conflicts affecting U.S. interests are likely to continue in Africa, the Middle East, Southwest Asia, and Latin America. . . .

Despite these and other dangers, it may be well to recall that . . . the conventional defense of Western Europe now costs the United States about $126 billion a year, of which no more than $22 billion has to do with maintaining a significant U.S. presence in Europe with $3\frac{2}{3}$ divisions and $7\frac{1}{3}$ fighter-attack wings.

To put the matter another way . . . the United States could save more than $500 billion during the coming decade if the military competition were replaced by a cooperative reduction of armaments.

Now that the Soviet leadership has recognized how much it has suffered from the competition, at least for now, and how high the cost has proved, an opportunity presents itself to put an end to the military contest and to the risks that have accompanied it.

*

"Only SDI can provide the technology for the types of defenses that will be necessary in the future."

The U.S. Should Invest in Advanced Laser Weapons

International Security Council

In 1983, U.S. president Ronald Reagan announced the Strategic Defense Initiative, a system of space-based laser weapons that would, if developed, protect the U.S. from incoming nuclear missiles. While SDI has remained controversial, debate concerning the future of SDI increased after the success of the Patriot missile, an SDI-type weapon, in the Persian Gulf War. In the following viewpoint, the International Security Council argues that the U.S. should invest in more SDI technology. The worldwide proliferation of nuclear and conventional missiles threatens the U.S., and space-based weapons can defend against such missiles, the council concludes. The International Security Council, a foreign policy and defense think tank in Washington, D.C., publishes the monthly journal *Global Affairs*.

As you read, consider the following questions:

1. What three realities did the Persian Gulf War demonstrate, in the council's opinion?
2. How did the Persian Gulf War refute the belief that there is no need for missile defense, according to the authors?
3. What does the council want Congress to do about SDI funding?

International Security Council, "SDI: Now More than Ever," *The Washington Times*, February 12, 1991. Reprinted with permission.

In an "Op-Ed" article published in *The New York Times* on May 16, 1990, the International Security Council focused on the threats posed by the proliferation of ballistic missiles in the hands of aggressor states and ruthless dictators, singling out in particular Iraq and Saddam Hussein. "The proliferation of missiles and warheads among irresponsible, aggressive states underscores the urgent need for missile defenses not only for Israel and other U.S. allies, but for the United States as well."

On January 18, 1991, the U.S. Army's Patriot missile intercepted an Iraqi Scud missile heading toward the U.S. airbase at Dhahran, Saudi Arabia. This Patriot intercept represented the first attempt in history to shoot down a ballistic missile in combat. And it was successful. The Patriot became world famous as it intercepted barrages of Iraqi Scuds bearing down on Israel and Saudi Arabia. British newspapers hailed the Patriot as "The Missile We Love." Greece and Turkey asked for the Patriot as vital to their security.

The Realities of Defense

Our experience in the war with Iraq demonstrated three realities beyond any doubt. The first is that not all missile attacks can be reliably deterred—not even by target states possessing nuclear weapons. . . .

Second, it is not always possible to destroy missiles prior to their launch. The United States and its allies in the Gulf were unable to locate and destroy all of the platforms, mobile or fixed, launching Scud missiles from Iraq despite six months of search and preparation. . . .

The third reality is that the technology to protect against missile attacks is in hand. The only obstacle to having and extending that capability is political.

Until recently, Patriot was limited to defending against aircraft; it was incapable of bringing down missiles such as the Soviet-made Scuds used by Iraq. Had the opponents of missile defense had their way, the recent improvements giving Patriot the capability to intercept missiles would have died on the drafting table, and there would have been nothing to stop Saddam Hussein's missiles from striking Israeli and Saudi civilians, and American military personnel in Saudi Arabia.

The Patriot system, it must be understood, is not representative of advanced SDI [Strategic Defense Initiative] ABM [antiballistic missile] technology, but of older technology and of very limited objectives. The Patriot was initially developed in the *1960s* as a dual-purpose air defense and anti-tactical missile defense, which was deliberately downgraded to strictly air defense in the early 1970s after the SALT [Strategic Arms Limitation Talks] ABM Treaty was concluded—even though the ABM

Treaty in no way prohibits the development and deployment of anti-tactical missile defenses. Later, it was decided to modify the system to enable it to defend itself, and still later to defend a limited area around the fire unit.

It is a sober commentary on the strength of congressional anti-ballistic missile defense opponents that our only missile defense capability to date had to be sold to Congress as an upgrade of an air defense system. Even at that, the program was barely kept alive. Had the Patriot been a true, dedicated anti-missile defense system, it is unlikely that Congress would have funded it.

A Commitment to Laser Technology

A wholehearted commitment to real defense can produce both ground-based and space-based lasers: directed energy weapons that destroy attacking missiles at the speed of light.

Missile technology and weapons of mass destruction are proliferating around the world. Mohammar Qadaffi of Libya said that if he had possessed a missile capable of reaching the U.S. during our air raid on Tripoli in 1986, he would have fired it at New York. Future aggressors may have the ability as well as the intent.

Thousands of Soviet nuclear warheads remain aimed at America. Who can guarantee that Mikhail Gorbachev or a successor will never launch an ICBM [intercontinental ballistic missile] or blackmail us with the threat of nuclear attack?

A first-generation missile defense based on existing technologies would not intercept every warhead, in the unlikely event the Soviets launched their entire arsenal. But it would limit the damage and save countless lives. And it could certainly stop a limited missile attack or stop missiles sent aloft in an unauthorized launch.

Malcolm Wallop, *New Dimensions,* May 1991.

Patriot worked well against Saddam's Scuds. But it is light-years short of the capability we *could* have had, and should now have, with SDI technology and a dedicated missile defense.

Critics Were Wrong

Critics of ABM have long argued that there is no need for missile defense, that defenses wouldn't work, that they would be too costly, or that they would be "destabilizing" and prevent more effective arms control solutions to the threat of ballistic missiles. The Gulf war has shown that the critics of missile defense have been wrong from the beginning, on all counts.

For example, the Gulf war brought home a point made by

SDI supporters for months: as missiles proliferate throughout the Third World, there simply will be no alternative to a U.S. capability to defend itself and its overseas forces and allies against ballistic missiles. Already, a dozen countries possess Scuds. Secretary of Defense [Richard] Cheney has projected that by the year 2000, 24 or more Third World countries will have ballistic missiles, 30 will have a chemical weapons capability, and as many as eight will have a nuclear capability. While most of the missiles now in the hands of these countries are of limited range and capability, the trend in proliferation is toward missiles with longer ranges and better accuracy: in short, greater strategic threats.

It is only a matter of time before the United States itself becomes vulnerable to this emerging threat of Third World ballistic missiles. It is now vulnerable to the very large and still expanding arsenal of Soviet intercontinental and submarine-launched ballistic missiles. The answer to the question, "Shouldn't Americans be protected at least as well as their allies?" is self-evident.

Opponents of missile defense have rejected the need for missile defenses based on an apparent faith that rationality and deterrence will work. Saddam Hussein demonstrated that rationality and the very credible threat of retaliation did not dissuade him from attacking Israel and American forces with his Scud missiles. Saddam Hussein also declared that, "Our missiles cannot reach Washington. If they could reach Washington, we would strike it if the need arose." Qadhaffi of Libya has made similar threats.

Traditional Deterrence Is Inadequate

Consequently, a clear lesson of the Gulf war is that the traditional U.S. reliance on deterrence and the threat of retaliation will not be adequate in the international environment of the 1990s and beyond. Defenses for U.S. forces and allies abroad and for the United States itself will be essential to American security.

Another lesson of the Gulf war is that even imperfect defenses are valuable. SDI critics frequently argue that if missile defenses are not 100 percent effective, they are useless. The impressive performance of Patriot revealed in human terms the value of even imperfect defenses, a value greatly appreciated by Israelis, Saudis, and American service men and women. As the Third World missile threat to the United States emerges in the 1990s, it is necessary only to picture Americans wearing gas masks and huddled in sealed rooms to appreciate the value of future defenses, even if they too are less than perfect. No one in Israel or Saudi Arabia is airing cost-benefit complaints against the Patriot, or suggesting that those hundreds, perhaps thousands of lives that Patriot saved are not worth the price of these "imperfect" defense systems. Nor is it likely that the beneficiaries of this protection, including our own men and women, deemed it "destabilizing."

Saddam's missile attacks and his longstanding missile development programs also demonstrated the inadequacy of arms control and technology transfer controls to prevent the emerging threat posed by the spread of missile technology. The ballistic missile genie is "out of the bottle," and the best that may be hoped for from such essentially voluntary controls is a slowing of proliferation.

A Clear Need for Missile Defense

The need for a missile defense capability is clear. The upgraded Patriot is designed to provide only a limited defense capability against short-range missiles such as the Scud. It would not provide protection against intercontinental ballistic missiles that threaten the United States, or against missiles with chemical or nuclear warheads that might detonate even if the missile were intercepted. Only SDI can provide the technology for the types of defenses that will be necessary in the future. And the SDI program is developing such a defense, called "GPALS," which stands for global protection against limited strikes. GPALS would use missile defense systems deployed on the ground—far more advanced and capable Patriot-type systems—and in space for more complete protection against threats from any quarter. The costs of GPALS, including theater as well as U.S. and space-based systems, would amount to no more than two or three percent of the defense budget for a few years.

Congress, however, slashed the administration's FY [fiscal year] 1991 SDI funding request by nearly $2 billion to only $2.9 billion, and seems determined to treat 1992's request similarly. These cuts virtually assure that America will remain defenseless against missile threats. It is time for Congress to understand what America needs and the American people want—and for the President to spell out the clear lessons of the Gulf war in terms of modest real costs and limitless real benefits. Congress should restore the SDI funds cut for 1991 and appropriate the entire funding request for 1992. And the administration should immediately get on with the task of deploying missile defenses, instead of merely researching the problem.

4
VIEWPOINT

"The Strategic Defense Initiative . . . has quietly received multibillion-dollar budgets each year, despite continued congressional and public skepticism about its feasibility."

The U.S. Should Not Invest in Advanced Laser Weapons

Jim Rice

Supporters of the Strategic Defense Initiative (SDI) point to the success of the Patriot missile as evidence that SDI technology is an effective and worthwhile investment. In the following viewpoint, Jim Rice refutes this assertion and argues that SDI is a wasteful program that can do nothing to protect America's security. Rice maintains that there is no relationship between the success of the Patriot and the feasibility of space-based SDI weapons. Rather than investing in more SDI research, Rice suggests that the U.S. invest in easing the social problems that lead to war. Rice is an assistant editor at *Sojourners,* a monthly magazine of religious, political, and social thought.

As you read, consider the following questions:

1. What is the real reason many politicians are linking the success of the Patriot to SDI, in the author's opinion?
2. What does Rice believe would be the real result of deploying SDI?
3. How can the world achieve security, in the author's opinion?

Jim Rice, "SDI-Lite: Old Wine in New Skins," *Sojourners,* May 1991. Reprinted with permission from *Sojourners,* PO Box 29272, Washington, DC 20017.

President Ronald Reagan's concept of a space shield that would render nuclear weapons "impotent and obsolete" was always a technological will-o'-the-wisp in the eyes of most credible scientists. But that hasn't made the Strategic Defense Initiative, or "Star Wars," go away; the program has quietly received multibillion-dollar budgets each year, despite continued congressional and public skepticism about its feasibility.

In late January 1991, the Bush administration—with the hopes of giving the Star Wars program a renewed lease on life—announced a new goal for the effort. In a clear attempt to cash in on the public perception of the success of the Patriot missiles in the Gulf war, the government proclaimed that the new Star Wars objective is to develop a system capable of protecting the United States and its military forces against a "limited" attack of fewer than 100 missiles.

Old Wine, New Skins

For some expert observers, however, the "new" Star Wars is just old wine in new skins. Peter Clausen, director of research for the Union of Concerned Scientists, maintains that despite its repackaging, the limited-objective system is "basically a downsized version of the misplaced approach that SDI has been pursuing for years."

And despite the shrunken goal, the cost has risen dramatically. Bush is seeking a 65 percent increase in 1992's SDI budget, to $5.2 billion. Why the sudden confidence that Congress will refund this lemon-in-the-sky program, especially in light of the shrinking budget pie? The answer is another legacy of the Gulf war.

In the eyes of SDI cheerleaders, Patriots knocking down Scuds has become an argument for Star Wars. White House Press Secretary Marlin Fitzwater said of the Patriot, "Its success does give us another degree of optimism about pursuing those kinds of technologies." Sen. Arlen Specter (R.-Pa.), a longtime Star Wars booster, said, "It shows it can work. It's a real shot in the arm for SDI."

Other observers, however, are convinced that the Patriot-ic argument is not really a military or technical one, but rather is a case of sheer political opportunism. "President Bush is trying to exploit the success of the Patriots to promote a program that has very little to do with Patriots," explained UCS media director Eileen Quinn. Former defense secretary Harold Brown said that linking the Patriots with Star Wars "is just partisan nonsense."

What would have happened, for example, if the Scuds were replaced with nuclear-tipped missiles? The allied barracks destroyed would have been a whole city annihilated. Modern ballistic missiles can be equipped with multiple, maneuvering warheads, decoy re-entry vehicles, and electronic devices to counter defenses—and they arrive at about 10,000 mph.

With Star Wars on the ropes, its supporters needed a new rationale to justify the continued expenditure of billions of dollars on a program that seemed obsolete with the demise of the Cold War. SDI officials in the recent past have disparaged limited or theater defenses in favor of the global space-based systems, and since 1984 only 5 percent of the $23 billion spent on SDI has been for systems designed for Scud-like tactical threats. Congress had to override administration objections in order to create a "Theater Missile Defense Initiative."

Toles. Copyright 1991 *The Buffalo News. Reprinted with permission of Universal Press Syndicate. All rights reserved.*

With bills pending in Congress that would transfer Patriot-type programs from the SDI office to the Army or the new theater initiative, the Star Wars program was threatened with extinction—and its backers adeptly changed their tune. The Pentagon is now attempting to sell the new "SDI-Lite" as protection against attack by a Third World nation or terrorist group. Such an attack, however, is unlikely to come via a ballistic missile—Clausen maintains that most Third World countries aren't likely to develop the sophisticated technology of a ballistic missile that could reach the United States for 50 years. Rather, a cruder delivery vehicle would more likely be used: a truck, a plane, or a boat—methods the $40 billion defense program wouldn't be able to stop.

The alleged change in Star Wars' purpose does not appear to be much more than a fund-raising smokescreen: The real long-term goal of SDI remains space-based weapons. A Defense Department news release promised that, if Congress provides the funds, the SDI office will "provide options to begin deployment by the late 1990s of ballistic missile defenses for the American people."

UCS' Clausen says that SDI advocates seem to have a "fixation" with space weapons. "It's an obsession they can't get rid of," Clausen said. "They take anything that comes along to try and justify it."

The Star Wars techno-shield, mythical or not, would provide one kind of protection: Deployment of such a system would eliminate the need, in the minds of many, to address the causes of conflict around the world. If technology makes you secure, there is no need for diplomacy. As columnist Mary McGrory wrote, "The Persian Gulf war, which was a piece of cake for our troops, could make war a seductive alternative to the tedious, repetitive work of diplomacy."

The Root Causes of War

But real security will never come from stockpiling weapons—whether they are termed offensive or defensive. In scripture, we are taught that the path to security is by necessity paved with justice and fairness. History has shown that weapons of mass destruction are not safe in human hands, as prone to conflict as we are. Only when such weapons are finally outlawed and the root causes of war are addressed—and the quixotic quest for techno-security abandoned—will the world begin to resolve its inevitable conflicts without resort to massive violence.

*"Until the Soviet Union changes a good deal
more . . . we will have to continue to rely on our
nuclear deterrent to ensure peace."*

The U.S. Must Maintain Its Nuclear Arsenal

Jon Kyl and F. Charles Gilbert

Many analysts have suggested that the U.S. can reduce its nuclear arsenal now that the Cold War is over. In the following
viewpoint, Jon Kyl and F. Charles Gilbert oppose this suggestion and argue that the U.S. will require strong nuclear defenses
as long as the Soviet Union continues to maintain its nuclear arsenal. Kyl is a U.S. congressman from Arizona. Gilbert is a fellow with the House Armed Services Committee and a former
deputy assistant secretary of the Department of Energy.

As you read, consider the following questions:

1. Why do the authors believe the Soviet Union may now pose
   a greater threat to the U.S. than ever before?
2. Why has the stockpile of nuclear weapons decreased in the
   last thirty years, according to Kyl and Gilbert?
3. What reasons do the authors give to support their belief that
   the U.S. should regularly rebuild its nuclear weapons
   arsenal?

Jon Kyl and F. Charles Gilbert, "Why Do We Still Need a Nuclear Deterrent?" *Forum for
Applied Research and Public Policy,* Spring 1991. Reprinted with permission.

In this period of relaxing tensions with the Soviet Union, when the East-Bloc nations are leaving the Warsaw Pact, when the Soviet economy is collapsing, and when the Soviet Union may be breaking apart, why do we still need a nuclear deterrent?

Because Soviet capabilities remain intact and intentions can change. No responsible defense planner relies solely on the expressed intentions of potential adversaries. The Soviet Union still has 30,000 nuclear weapons aimed directly at pre-selected targets in the United States—cities as well as military targets.

The danger that some of those weapons may be unleashed may be greater in this period of internal Soviet turmoil than during the previous 45 years when the country was ruled by malevolent but rational leaders.

A Need for Deterrence

For more than 40 years, the United States has relied on its nuclear retaliatory capability as a deterrent to attack. Until the Soviet Union changes a good deal more or until the United States has deployed strategic defenses, we will have to continue to rely on our nuclear deterrent to ensure peace. And, as other nations acquire ballistic missile capability and nuclear technology, this need will only increase.

Now that the thaw with the Soviet Union has begun, however, the U.S. government is struggling to maintain its nuclear deterrent in the face of environmental, political, and economic pressures that are threatening to weaken it. For the past 30 years, while Soviet nuclear forces have increased significantly, the U.S. stockpile has decreased by roughly 25 percent and its total explosive yield by roughly 75 percent.

This has come about partly because of the Intermediate-range Nuclear Forces (INF) Treaty but mostly because of technical improvements in warheads and their delivery systems. These improvements have allowed reductions in numbers and yields to accomplish the same mission. A further mutual and balanced reduction of 15 to 20 percent will occur if the United States signs a Strategic Arms Reduction Treaty (START) with the Soviets.

The Soviets may never have to sign that treaty, or any other nuclear-weapons treaty, however, if the United States cannot resume operations of its decrepit nuclear-weapons complex.

Rebuilding Weapons

To maintain a deterrent, the United States must regularly rebuild its weapons for several important reasons:

• *Aging.* Nuclear weapons are like automobiles; they age, even when they are not used. The rubber rots, the plastics become brittle, the metals corrode, the materials decompose (high explosives) and decay (tritium), and the glue that holds them together cracks and separates.

• *Safety.* Through the use of modern computers and nuclear testing, the safety of nuclear weapons is constantly improving. Such improvements are incorporated into new weapon systems, including better ways to prevent nuclear or non-nuclear explosions caused by accidents or unauthorized tampering.

Caution Is Needed

So great has been the reduction in Soviet-American tensions that there is once again a lot of loose talk about shutting down America's nuclear weapons program. That's exactly what some groups within the resurgent nuclear freeze movement would like the U.S. government to do.

They couldn't be more wrong—or, for that matter, more destructive to the arms control process. . . .

Caution must remain the watchword when dealing with the Soviet Union. As long as nuclear weapons exist, we will need to deter their use. Recent negotiations have shown that any serious discussion of arms control issues with the Soviets must be approached from a position of strength.

Mackubin Thomas Owens, *The Union Leader,* July 3, 1990.

• *Security.* To prevent unauthorized use of nuclear weapons, coded locks, called permissive action links, are built into each new U.S. nuclear weapon. These safeguards have become more effective with modern electronics. Weapons should be equipped with the best lock-out devices available to prevent terrorists or other malevolent individuals from detonating a nuclear weapon.

• *Changing Requirements.* Military systems must change to meet new threats or because improved delivery systems become available—new aircraft (B-1), missiles (MX), or submarines (Trident-II). Old warheads cannot always be adapted to fit the new systems.

The Complex Today

When the United States built the nuclear-weapons complex in the 1940s and 1950s, there was considerable concern over its vulnerability. Critical plants were duplicated for backup and distributed over the entire United States. This redundancy is gone, but the broad geographic distribution of the facilities remains. The current nuclear-weapons complex consists of 16 principal facilities distributed around the United States. . . .

The weapons complex suffers from what every large industry eventually faces: obsolescence, oversize, poor location, aging work force, and outdated production techniques. If the complex were a private industry, it would have to either invest heavily in modernization to stay competitive or lose out to a more efficient competitor. However, the government doesn't work that way. . . .

The complex is currently too large, too old, too spread out, too inefficient and, above all, it does not meet modern environmental and safety standards. . . .

Modernizing the weapons production complex will be long and difficult, but necessary. . . .

Even if the United States achieves substantial nuclear arms-reduction agreements with the Soviet Union, it will be vital to maintain a credible deterrent, not only with respect to the Soviets but also with respect to emerging Third-World countries whose ambitions may threaten the United States.

"The cloistered world of strategic theory can no longer ignore the overwhelming, popular desires for deep reductions in nuclear weapons."

The U.S. Must Consider Reducing Its Nuclear Arsenal

John Tirman

The U.S. should reconsider its nuclear weapons policy, John Tirman argues in the following viewpoint. Tirman states that the U.S. is maintaining its nuclear arsenal as if the Cold War still exists. He argues that it is time the U.S. government responded to the desires of the American public and considered reducing the nation's nuclear arsenal. Tirman is executive director of the Winston Foundation for World Peace in Boston.

As you read, consider the following questions:

1. What does the author believe is the Bush administration's stance on nuclear weapons?
2. How does Tirman refute the arguments for the counterforce doctrine?
3. What role can the Conference on Security and Cooperation play in the protection of the U.S. and its allies, in the author's opinion?

John Tirman, "Rethinking Deterrence," *Nuclear Times,* Autumn 1990. Reprinted with permission.

Nothing more sharply defined the Cold War era than nuclear weapons and the fitful attempts to contain their growth. With the demise of the U.S.-Soviet confrontation, this unique feature is likely to change. But there is nothing preordained about how the new detente, the collapse of communism, or the relative decline of both nations will affect the theory and practice of nuclear deterrence.

The Strategic Arms Reduction Treaty (START) signals a new period of progress, as do the negotiations to reduce conventional forces in Europe. Soviet troops in Eastern Europe were a principal rationale for a sizable nuclear deterrent in the West, but significant cuts in Soviet forces are underway as new governments in Czechoslovakia and Hungary have requested their removal. The unification of Germany will hasten the Soviet departure.

These changes are nothing short of revolutionary in the political, social, and economic life of Central Europe and in the West's ties to those countries. But will nuclear doctrine follow suit? How is the Gorbachev phenomenon affecting the thinking of America's defense intelligentsia?

The Bush administration is clearly wedded to the status quo: supporting strategic modernization; the Star Wars program, which has a new, enthusiastic chief; and a new nuclear warfighting plan installed in October 1989 that a leading expert calls "wasteful and dangerous . . . as well as destabilizing." Arms control has new life, but the START accord offers only small cuts, while the administration resists naval arms control, a nuclear test ban, space arms restrictions, and other signs of genuine change. . . .

Signs of Change

At present, signs of a shift in U.S. strategic thinking are barely evident, and those appear to be budget driven. "Some 'establishment' thinkers have proposed major changes in forces," notes Stephen Van Evera, an MIT [Massachusetts Institute of Technology] professor and former editor of the influential journal *International Security.* "In particular, Lawrence Korb and William Kaufmann [both former Pentagon officials] have been willing to cut the budget by 50 percent over the next decade, very big cuts when compared with the administration's proposals. However, these are reductions commensurate with the level of threat, not necessarily a change in doctrine. Compared with thinkers in the Soviet Union—who now say there is no threat from the West, and who favor a dramatic shift to a more defensive military doctrine—a change in American doctrinal thinking is not perceptible.". . .

"What has driven both sides to larger arsenals has been the 'need' to cover the other side's forces, resulting in an endless, mutual expansion," explains Van Evera. "With both sides believing in counterforce, arsenals had to grow. It's an 'impossible' doctrine, because its requirements can never be met."

Counterforce doctrine calls for nuclear strikes against nuclear forces, rather than civilian or industrial targets, in order to disable the adversary's military capability first. That requires very accurate weapons, such as the MX and Trident II missiles, and is bolstered by strategic defenses, such as SDI [Strategic Defense Initiative], which further compromise the adversary's offensive power. . . .

"Can't you see that if we don't use those bombs it's all a waste of money?"

Counterforce was always hotly debated; critics charge it is unnecessary, provocative, and possibly catastrophic. During the Cold War, proponents argued that counterforce was needed for four reasons. First, to prevent the Soviet Union from carrying out its own war plan, which included destruction of U.S. cities. Second, to deter Soviets by threatening things they cared about (i.e., Communist Party leaders). Third, to bankrupt the USSR with an arms race. And fourth, to provide "extended deterrence" to Europe.

The demise of the Cold War undermines those arguments. The first—the need to preempt a Soviet nuclear attack—was built on an unprovable faith in first-strike capability and equivocation about U.S. intentions. The other three are vitiated by the Gorbachev phenomenon, the new detente, and the near-total retreat of the USSR from Eastern Europe. "None of these reasons for counterforce are operative now," says Van Evera, "yet strategists are not reexamining this.". . .

Return to Basics

At a time of sweeping change, a healthy urge to reassess the nation's direction takes hold of many analysts. The questions are now well known: Can America continue to police the world, given shifts in economic power and the decline of Soviet communism as an adversary? If not, what sort of global role should America adopt? . . .

New forms of common security are now more viable than ever if given the time and commitment to work, and the acceptance of these promising arrangements would signal a shift in U.S. thinking that should affect nuclear doctrine.

Chief among the near-term possibilities is the Conference on Security and Cooperation in Europe (CSCE), a 35-nation process that ushered in the Helsinki accords in 1975. Many Europeans, including Gorbachev, regard CSCE as the security framework of the future precisely because it includes the Warsaw Pact. An empowered CSCE would, of course, render NATO [North Atlantic Treaty Organization] little more than an artifact of the Cold War. According to [the Brookings Institution's] Raymond Garthoff, "from the Soviet point of view, the United States has not seemed to be prepared to move toward accepting this idea of a genuine East-West security framework." The "new Europe" is a hot topic within intellectual circles, and this may filter into broader questions of nuclear policy. Indeed, how the United States regards CSCE will be another litmus test of new thinking.

START 2 and CSCE will be the most public displays of U.S. direction on security and nuclear deterrence. But the workings of arms control and the building of new security structures are slow and rarely conclusive. Many strategists in and out of government will cling to old notions of nuclear superiority and counterforce as the linchpins of U.S. policy. "Losers learn a lot more from history that winners do," says MIT's Van Evera. "Nothing focuses the mind like the failure of long-cherished policy. Winners are complacent. It's like, 'We won, and we're cool.'

"Throughout the Cold War not enough questions were raised in the defense community about official beliefs. Today we're seeing a continuation of that. We don't have a debate about roles and mission, and the military is loathe to talk about that—secrecy is to their advantage."

It may be, however, that the cloistered world of strategic theory can no longer ignore the overwhelming, popular desires for deep reductions in nuclear weapons and new, more cooperative security arrangements.

a critical thinking activity

Understanding Words in Context

Readers occasionally come across words they do not recognize. And frequently, because they do not know a word or words, they will not fully understand the passage being read. Obviously, the reader can look up an unfamiliar word in a dictionary. By carefully examining the word in the context in which it is used, however, the word's meaning can often be determined. A careful reader may find clues to the meaning of the word in surrounding words, ideas, and attitudes.

Below are excerpts from the viewpoints in this chapter. In each excerpt, one of the words is printed in italics. Try to determine the meaning of each word by reading the excerpt. Under each excerpt you will find four definitions for the italicized word. Choose the one that is closest to your understanding of the word.

Finally, use a dictionary to see how well you have understood the words in context. It will be helpful to discuss with others the clues that helped you decide on each word's meaning.

1. Rather than waiting for Iraq to invade Saudi Arabia, Allied forces took a *PREEMPTIVE* measure and attacked Iraqi forces before they crossed into the desert nation.

   PREEMPTIVE means:

   a) self-initiated   c) full
   b) foolish   d) uninformed

2. By encouraging the two nations to reduce their number of weapons to the same level, the negotiators helped establish *PARITY* between the superpowers' defense capabilities.

   PARITY means:

   a) disunity   c) goals
   b) equality   d) simplicity

3. The *METRONOMIC* precision of the weapon was evident by its constant, repeated firing.

METRONOMIC means:

a) advanced   c) simple
b) unsatisfactory   d) rhythmic

4. Their long history of conflict makes the nations of the Middle East potential *BELLIGERENTS* who pose a constant threat to world peace.

BELLIGERENTS means:

a) operators   c) negotiators
b) warmongers   d) peacemakers

5. Arms dealers are responsible for the *PROLIFERATION* of missiles and warheads among irresponsible, aggressive Third World nations.

PROLIFERATION means:

a) storing   c) spread
b) firing   d) destruction

6. Upon impact, the bomb *DETONATED* and destroyed the bridge.

DETONATED means:

a) fizzled   c) deactivated
b) bounced   d) exploded

7. If Iraq's Scud missiles had contained nuclear bombs, the entire city of Tel Aviv would have been *ANNIHILATED.*

ANNIHILATED means:

a) destroyed   c) disrupted
b) protected   d) altered

8. For more than forty years, the U.S. has relied on its nuclear *RETALIATORY CAPABILITY* as a deterrent to attack.

RETALIATORY CAPABILITY means:

a) ability to make peace   c) ability to sell for less than retail
b) ability to repay in kind   d) ability to be calm

9. The weapons industry, which uses old technology and equipment, suffers from *OBSOLESCENCE.*

OBSOLESCENCE means:

a) fatigue   c) helplessness
b) outdatedness   d) indebtedness

Periodical Bibliography

The following articles have been selected to supplement the diverse views presented in this chapter.

David Albright and Tom Zamora	"How Big an Arsenal Does U.S. Need Now?" *Forum for Applied Research and Public Policy,* Spring 1991. Available from the University of North Carolina Press, PO Box 2288, Chapel Hill, NC 27515-2288.
Stephen Aubin	"The Patriot and SDI: Changing Images," *The World & I,* May 1991.
Fred Barnes	"Brilliant Pebble," *The New Republic,* April 1, 1991.
Ralph Kinney Bennett	"Defenseless Against Missile Terror," *Reader's Digest,* October 1990.
Tom Bethell	"Star-Wars Wars," *The American Spectator,* April 1991.
Stephen Budiansky	"Overtaking Arms Control," *U.S. News & World Report,* June 11, 1990.
W. Seth Carus	"Missiles in the Third World: The 1991 Gulf War," *Orbis,* Spring 1991.
Angelo Codevilla	"A Question of Patriot-ism," *Policy Review,* Spring 1991.
Jeffrey Denny	"Star Struck," *Common Cause Magazine,* March/April 1991.
Philip Elmer-Dewitt	"Inside the High-Tech Arsenal," *Time,* February 4, 1991.
T.A. Heppenheimer	"Surgical Strikes," *Reason,* April 1991.
Michael T. Klare	"High-Death Weapons of the Gulf War," *The Nation,* June 3, 1991.
Ed Magnuson	"Misplaced Priorities," *Time,* April 8, 1991.
Peter Montgomery	"Re-arm the World," *Common Cause Magazine,* May/June 1991.
Janne E. Nolan	"Who Decides?" *Technology Review,* January 1991.
Otis Port et al.	"Suddenly, All Eyes Are on Stealth," *Business Week,* March 25, 1991.
Virginia Postrel	"Cybernetic War," *Reason,* April 1991.

Chronology of Twentieth-Century U.S. Military Actions

1900	U.S. troops help suppress Boxer Rebellion in China.
1909	U.S. troops intervene in Nicaragua after overthrow of dictator Jose Santos Zelaya.
1912	U.S. Marines sent to Nicaragua.
1914	U.S. Atlantic Fleet occupies Veracruz, Mexico, after U.S. soldiers are arrested in Tampico.
1915	U.S. troops sent to Haiti. Treaty puts Haiti under U.S. protection.
1916	U.S. forces under Gen. John J. Pershing enter Mexico to pursue Pancho Villa, Mexican revolutionary and bandit.
1917	U.S. declares war with Germany on April 6. First U.S. troops arrive in Europe on June 26.
1918	World War I ends. More than one million U.S. troops stationed in Europe. A small American force occupies Archangel and Murmansk in the northern Soviet Union to support local anticommunist forces against the Bolsheviks.
1927	To protect American property during China's civil war, about one thousand U.S. Marines are sent to China. U.S. Marines occupy Nicaragua when Gen. Augusto C. Sandino refuses to accept the peace accord between the government and his revolutionaries. Sandino leads his guerrillas against U.S. Marines.
1933	U.S. Marines withdraw from Nicaragua after appointment of Gen. Anastasio Somoza Garcia as president.
1934	U.S. troops withdraw from Haiti.
1939	U.S. declares its neutrality as World War II begins.
1941	U.S. occupies Iceland on July 7. Japan attacks Pearl Harbor, Hawaii, on December 7, destroying or damaging nineteen ships and killing twenty-three hundred. U.S. declares war on Japan, Germany, and Italy.
1942	U.S. forces defeat Japan in the Battle of Midway in June and land on Guadalcanal in August. U.S. and British forces invade North Africa in November.
1943	U.S. troops invade Italy.
1944	U.S. and Allied forces invade France at Normandy.
1945	U.S. Marines invade Iwo Jima and Okinawa. Germany surrenders. U.S. drops atomic bombs on Hiroshima and Nagasaki, Japan. Japan surrenders. U.S. and Soviet forces occupy Korea.
1947	Pres. Harry Truman announces the containment doctrine, aimed at preventing communist expansion in Europe.
1949	U.S. troops withdraw from Korea. North Atlantic Treaty Organization (NATO) established by U.S.,

Canada, and ten Western European nations to ensure a common defense.

1950	Truman orders U.S. air and naval forces to attack North Korea after it invades South Korea. U.S. soldiers land at Inchon. The U.S. sends military advisors to Vietnam and agrees to supply the nation with military and economic aid.
1953	After two years of cease-fire talks, the Korean conflict ends.
1954	The U.S., Britain, France, Australia, New Zealand, Philippines, Pakistan, and Thailand form the Southeast Asia Treaty Organization (SEATO) for common defense.
1955	U.S. advisors begin training the South Vietnamese army.
1958	The U.S. sends five thousand marines to Lebanon to protect the elected government from a possible coup.
1960	U.S. pilot Francis Gary Powers shot down in his U-2 reconnaissance plane over the Soviet Union. The incident increases the tension and distrust between the two nations.
1961	U.S. invasion of Cuba's Bay of Pigs fails. The U.S. had trained, armed, and directed Cuban exiles in an attempt to overthrow the regime of Fidel Castro.
1962	The U.S. discovers Soviet missiles in Cuba. Pres. John F. Kennedy orders a naval and air blockade of Cuba to prevent further Soviet military shipments to the island. The Soviets dismantle the missile bases. Two U.S. Army air support companies arrive in Saigon. U.S. troops in South Vietnam total four thousand.
1963	More than 15,000 U.S. troops stationed in Vietnam.
1964	U.S. announces that it sent military planes to Laos. The U.S. Congress passes the Gulf of Tonkin Resolution, which gives Pres. Lyndon Baines Johnson more authority in the Vietnam conflict.
1965	Johnson orders the continuous bombing of North Vietnam below the 20th parallel. American troops in South Vietnam total 184,300. U.S. sends 14,000 troops to Dominican Republic to restore order during that nation's civil war.
1966	U.S. troops begin firing into Cambodia in an attempt to attack North Vietnamese bases. U.S. begins bombing of Hanoi. U.S. troops in South Vietnam total 385,300.
1967	U.S. expands bombing to include all of North Vietnam. U.S. troops in South Vietnam total 475,000.
1968	The USS *Pueblo* is seized by North Korea in the Sea of Japan. The crew is released eleven months later. Communist troops attack Saigon, in what becomes known as the Tet Offensive. U.S. and South Vietnamese troops defeat the Communists. Johnson halts all bombing of North Vietnam.
1969	U.S. begins withdrawing forces from Vietnam. Before withdrawal, U.S. troops in South Vietnam totaled

543,400.

1970	U.S. and South Vietnamese troops cross into Cambodia to locate North Vietnamese bases. U.S. Senate repeals the 1964 Gulf of Tonkin Resolution.
1971	The U.S. uses its air and artillery forces to assist South Vietnamese forces in an attack on Laos.
1972	North Vietnamese forces launch major attacks across the demilitarized zone. The U.S. resumes bombing of Hanoi and Haiphong, and mines North Vietnamese ports. The U.S. and the Soviet Union conclude the SALT I agreements, which set a ceiling of two hundred antiballistic missiles for both sides and freeze Soviet ICBMs at 1,618 and U.S. ICBMs at 1,054.
1973	The U.S., South Vietnam, North Vietnam, and the Viet Cong sign peace agreements, including a ceasefire and a withdrawal of U.S. troops. U.S. troops leave South Vietnam. The U.S. ends bombing in Cambodia. Congress overrides Pres. Richard Nixon's veto of the War Powers Resolution, which limits the president's authority to wage war without Congressional approval.
1975	The U.S. merchant ship *Mayaguez* is seized by Cambodian forces in the Gulf of Siam. In response, U.S. Marines attack Tang Island and U.S. planes bomb the island's air base. Cambodia surrenders the ship and its crew. Pres. Gerald Ford declares the Vietnam conflict over.
1977	Fifteen nations, including the U.S. and the Soviet Union, sign a nuclear nonproliferation pact.
1979	The SALT II agreement is signed by Pres. Jimmy Carter and Soviet leader Leonid Brezhnev; the U.S. refuses final ratification after the Soviets invade Afghanistan.
1980	Eight Americans are killed and five wounded in a failed attempt to rescue American hostages held by Iranian terrorists at the U.S. Embassy in Tehran. The U.S. sends military advisors to El Salvador to aid the Salvadoran government against leftist rebels.
1983	A terrorist blows up the U.S. Marine headquarters in Beirut, Lebanon, killing 241 marines and sailors, members of a multinational peacekeeping force. U.S. Marines and Army Rangers, with a small force from six Caribbean nations, invade the island of Grenada to rescue U.S. citizens and overthrow the Marxist regime. American troops leave after a pro-U.S. government is installed. Pres. Ronald Reagan proposes an antiballistic missile defense system, later to be named the Strategic Defense Initiative. The U.S. starts deploying cruise missiles in Europe, causing the Soviets to break off arms negotiations with the U.S.
1984	Reagan removes U.S. Marines from Beirut, stationing them on ships offshore. The Central Intelligence Agency mines Nicaragua's harbors in a covert operation. This action leads the World Court in 1986 to

find the U.S. guilty of violating international law.

1986	Libya launches missiles at a U.S. fleet on maneuvers in the Gulf of Sidra. U.S. missiles damage the Libyan missile site and destroy two patrol boats. U.S. planes bomb Tripoli and Benghazi, Libya, in retaliation for the Libyan bombing of a West Berlin disco.
	The U.S. House of Representatives permits the CIA and the Pentagon to train the Nicaraguan contras. A plane carrying U.S. military supplies to the contras is shot down in Nicaragua. The U.S. government announces it has been providing military aid to the contras, contrary to the Boland Amendment. The supplies were purchased with funds diverted from the sale of U.S. arms to Iran. The covert operation becomes known as the Iran-contra affair.
1987	An Iraqi missile kills thirty-seven sailors on the frigate USS *Stark* in the Persian Gulf. Iraq calls it an accident, and the ship's officers are found to have been negligent. The U.S. escorts Kuwaiti oil tankers to the Persian Gulf, reflagging them as U.S. ships.
1988	Reagan orders thirty-two hundred U.S. troops to Honduras after reports that two thousand Sandinistas have crossed into Honduras to attack a contra base. U.S. troops withdraw two weeks later.
	U.S. Navy warship *Vincennes* in the Persian Gulf destroys a commercial Iranian airliner, killing all aboard. U.S. Navy personnel mistook the airliner for an Iranian F-14 fighter.
1989	U.S. forces invade Panama and oust Panamanian leader Manuel Noriega.
1990	
August	U.S. Marines land in Liberia and evacuate 125 American citizens threatened by the West African nation's violent civil war.
	In response to the Iraqi invasion of Kuwait on August 2, the U.S. sends troops to Saudi Arabia on August 7 to deter Iraq from capturing the oil-rich fields of Saudi Arabia and to force Iraq to leave Kuwait. U.S. forces are joined by troops from other nations. The buildup of troops continues to the end of 1990.
1991	
January	U.S. and Allied air forces attack military targets in Iraq and Kuwait after the passing of the January 15 deadline imposed on Iraq by the United Nations.
February	U.S. and Allied forces launch a full-scale ground war against Iraqi forces in Kuwait. Allied forces push Iraqi forces out of Kuwait and into southern Iraq.
March	Iraq agrees to United Nation's conditions for a permanent cease-fire. The Persian Gulf War lasted forty-three days, with a ground war of one hundred hours. The Allies lost 141 soldiers; the Iraqis, between ten thousand and twenty thousand.

Organizations to Contact

The editors have compiled the following list of organizations that are concerned with the issues debated in this book. All of them have publications or information available for interested readers. The descriptions are derived from materials provided by the organizations. This list was compiled upon the date of publication. Names and phone numbers of organizations are subject to change.

American Defense Institute
1055 N. Fairfax St., 2d Fl.
Alexandria, VA 22314
(703) 519-7000

The institute is a nonprofit educational organization that supports a strong national defense. Its goal is to educate Americans concerning their national heritage and their freedoms. The institute publishes the quarterly newsletter *American Defense Initiative* as well as occasional articles.

American Enterprise Institute for Public Policy Research (AEI)
1150 17th St. NW
Washington, DC 20036
(202) 862-5800

AEI is a conservative research and education organization that studies national and international issues. It promotes the spread of democracy and a strong military to protect against the spread of totalitarianism. AEI publishes the monthly *AEI Economist*, the bimonthly *Public Opinion*, and various books on America's defense.

American Friends Service Committee
1501 Cherry St.
Philadelphia, PA 19102
(215) 241-7000

The committee is a Quaker organization that seeks better international relations through peace and pacifism. It opposes U.S. intervention in other nations' affairs. Its purpose is to relieve human suffering and to find new approaches to world peace through nonviolent social change. The committee publishes the monthly magazine *Friends Journal*.

American Security Council Foundation
Washington Communications Center
Box 8
Boston, VA 22713
(703) 547-1776

The foundation is a nonprofit research institute that studies national defense issues. The foundation supports a strong national defense. It publishes the newsletter *National Security Report* and policy papers and briefings.

The Brookings Institution
1175 Massachusetts Ave. NW
Washington, DC 20036
(202) 797-6000

The institution, founded in 1927, is a think tank that studies defense, foreign policy, government, and economics. It publishes the quarterly *Brookings Review*, the biannual *Brookings Papers on Economic Activity*, and various books.

Cato Institute
224 Second St. SE
Washington, DC 20003
(202) 546-0200

The institute is a public policy research foundation that researches defense and foreign policy issues as well as domestic issues such as education and health care. Several of its publications have addressed issues such as defense spending and the role of America's military in world affairs. The institute publishes the bimonthly *Policy Report* and the *Cato Journal* three times a year.

Center for Defense Information (CDI)
1500 Massachusetts Ave. NW
Washington, DC 20005
(202) 862-0700

CDI analyzes military spending, policies, and weapons systems. CDI's staff includes retired admirals, generals, and other former military officers, as well as civilians with extensive experience in military analysis. Its goals are to eliminate waste in military spending, to reduce the military's influence on U.S. domestic and foreign policy, and to prevent nuclear war. The center publishes *The Defense Monitor* ten times a year and sponsors the television program "America's Defense Monitor."

Committee on the Present Danger
905 16th St. NW, Suite 207
Washington, DC 20006
(202) 628-2409

The committee's goal is to inform the American public about the military capabilities of the Soviet Union. It contends that the Soviet Union's continuing advantage in military force threatens U.S. national security. The committee publishes the occasional periodical *The U.S.-Soviet Military Balance* in addition to books such as *Alerting America.*

Council on Foreign Relations
58 E. 68th St.
New York, NY 10021
(212) 734-0400

The council is a group of individuals with specialized knowledge of and interest in foreign affairs. It was formed to study the international aspects of American strategic, political, and economic problems. The council publishes *Foreign Affairs,* a well-known foreign-policy journal that covers a broad range of topics, including the role of America's military in world affairs.

Fellowship of Reconciliation (FOR/USA)
Box 271
Nyack, NY 10960
(914) 358-4601
FOR/USA is the American branch of a worldwide pacifist group organized at the beginning of World War I. Members seek to settle international disputes through nonviolence. FOR publishes *Fellowship* magazine eight times a year.

Foreign Policy Association
729 Seventh Ave.
New York, NY 10019
(212) 764-4050

The association, established in 1918, provides information designed to help citizens participate in foreign policy decisions. It does not take sides. It publishes the *Headline Series* of pamphlets and the annual report *Great Decisions*.

The Heritage Foundation
214 Massachusetts Ave. NE
Washington, DC 20002
(202) 546-4400

The foundation is a conservative think tank that favors a strong national defense. It supports U.S. military action to protect American interests and promote democratic movements in other nations. Among its many publications are the Heritage Foundation *Backgrounder*, *Lectures*, and the quarterly *Policy Review*.

Institute for Policy Studies
1601 Connecticut Ave. NW, Suite 500
Washington, DC 20009
(202) 234-9382

The institute's national security program provides factual analyses and critiques of America's military and foreign affairs policies. Its goal is to provide a balanced view of international relations. The institute publishes books, reports, and briefs.

Jobs with Peace
76 Summer St.
Boston, MA 02110

Jobs with Peace is a national campaign to reduce military spending and invest the money in housing, health care, child care, education, mass transit, and the environment. The organization publishes the newsletter *Campaign Report* twice a year in addition to fact sheets such as *We Need Homes Not Bombs*.

National Commission for Economic Conversion and Disarmament
1801 18th St. NW, Suite 9
Washington, DC 20009
(202) 462-0091

The commission advocates decreasing America's defense spending and using the savings to ease social problems such as poverty and homelessness. It publishes the newsletter *The New Economy* five times a year and periodic monographs and briefing papers such as *How the Military-serving Firm Differs from the Rest*, *An Introduction to Economic Conversion*, and *A Future for America and Its Cities: The Peace Dividend and Economic Conversion*.

United States Defense Committee
3238 Wynford Dr.
Fairfax, VA 22031
(703) 280-4226

The committee supports a strong national defense for the U.S. It lobbies Congress on defense issues. Publications of the committee include the bimonthly *Defense Watch* as well as defense briefs.

U.S. Department of Defense
Public Correspondence Division, Defense Information Services
Assistant Secretary of Defense, The Pentagon
Washington, DC 20301-1400
(703) 545-6700

The Department of Defense is responsible for providing the military forces needed to deter war and protect the security of the U.S. It also develops strategic plans to protect the U.S. and U.S. interests abroad. Write for a list of publications.

U.S. Department of State
Office of Public Communications, Public Information Service
Bureau of Public Affairs
Washington, DC 20520
(202) 647-6575

The Department of State advises the president in the formulation and execution of foreign policy. It publishes speeches and testimonies by government officials. Write or call for a list of publications.

United States Strategic Institute
2020 Pennsylvania Ave. NW, Suite 610
Washington, DC 20006
(202) 331-1776

The institute is a conservative think tank that studies political and military topics and U.S. national security policy. It publishes the quarterly journal *Strategic Review.*

Women's International League for Peace and Freedom (WILPF)
1213 Race St.
Philadelphia, PA 19107
(215) 563-7110

WILPF is an international network of women activists, with one hundred branches in the U.S. The league opposes militarism and U.S. intervention in other nations' affairs, and promotes disarmament. WILPF publishes the bimonthly magazine *Peace and Freedom* and the book *The Women's Budget*, which proposes a 50 percent cut in military expenditures and proposes redistributing those funds to social programs that benefit women and children.

Women's Research and Education Institute (WREI)
1700 18th St. NW, Suite 400
Washington, DC 20009
(202) 328-7070

WREI is an independent, national public policy research organization that studies women's issues. It manages an ongoing project on women in the military. The institute publishes frequent reports and analyses concerning women's issues, including *Women in the Military, 1980-1990* and *Women in the Armed Services: The War in the Persian Gulf*, and the book *The American Women.*

World Policy Institute
777 United Nations Plaza
New York, NY 10017
(212) 490-0010

The institute, affiliated with the New School for Social Research in New York City, is a public policy research organization that studies national security issues and foreign affairs. It supports decreased defense spending. Publications of the institute include the quarterly *World Policy Journal* and periodic reports.

Bibliography of Books

John J. Abt	*Who Has the Right to Make War? The Constitutional Crisis.* New York: International Publishers, 1970.
James Adams	*Engines of War: Merchants of Death and the New Arms Race.* New York: Atlantic Monthly Press, 1990.
Kenneth A. Adelman	*The Defense Revolution: Strategy for a Brave New World.* Washington, DC: Institute for Contemporary Studies, 1991.
Kenneth A. Adelman and Norman R. Augustine	*The Defense Revolution: Memos for the Brave New World by an Arms Controller and an Arms Builder.* San Francisco: ICS Press, 1990.
Carol Barkalow with Andrea Raab	*In the Men's House: An Inside Account of Life in the Army by One of West Point's First Female Graduates.* New York: Poseidon, 1990.
James A. Blackwell Jr. and Barry M. Blechman, eds.	*Making Defense Reform Work.* Washington, DC: Pergamon-Brassey's, 1990.
James R. Blaker	*United States Overseas Basing: An Anatomy of a Dilemma.* New York: Praeger, 1990.
Ted Galen Carpenter	*Collective Defense or Strategic Independence.* Lexington, MA: Lexington Books, 1989.
Philip C. Clarke	*The Missile Race: Why We Need Space Defense.* New Rochelle, NY: America's Future, Inc., 1991.
Jean Bethke Elshtain	*Women and War.* New York: Basic Books, 1987.
Jean Bethke Elshtain and Sheila Tobias	*Women, Militarism, and War: Essays in History, Politics, and Social Theory.* Savage, MD: Rowman & Littlefield, 1990.
Cynthia Enloe	*Does Khaki Become You? The Militarisation of Women's Lives.* Boston: South End Press, 1983.
James J. Frelk and Glen E. Tait, eds.	*Defending Against Ballistic Missile Attacks.* Washington, DC: George C. Marshall Institute, 1990.
Paul Fussell	*The Norton Book of Modern War.* New York: Norton, 1990.
Erhard Geissler, ed.	*Strengthening the Biological Weapons Convention by Confidence-building Measures.* Oxford: Oxford University Press, 1990.
Joseph Gerson and Bruce Birchard, eds.	*The Sun Never Sets: Confronting the Network of Foreign and U.S. Military Bases.* Boston: South End Press, 1991.
Fen Hampson	*Unguided Missiles: How America Buys Its Weapons.* New York: Norton, 1989.
William Darryl Henderson	*The Hollow Army.* Westport, CT: Greenwood Press, 1990.
Robert Higgs, ed.	*Arms, Politics, and the Economy.* Oakland, CA: The Independent Institute, 1990.
Jeanne Holm	*Women in the Military: An Unfinished Revolution.* Novato, CA: Presidio Press, 1982.

International Institute for Strategic Studies	*The Military Balance, 1990-1991.* London: Pergamon-Brassey's, 1990.
Joint Center for Political Studies	*Who Defends America? Race, Sex, and Class in the Armed Forces.* Washington, DC: Joint Center for Political Studies, 1989.
Jeane J. Kirkpatrick	*The Withering Away of the Totalitarian State . . . and Other Surprises.* Washington, DC: American Enterprise Institute for Public Policy Research, 1990.
Lawrence Margolis	*Executive Agreements and Presidential Power in Foreign Policy.* New York: Praeger, 1986.
Robert S. McNamara	*Out of the Cold: New Thinking for American Foreign and Defense Policy in the Twenty-first Century.* New York: Simon and Schuster, 1989.
Thomas L. McNaugher	*New Weapons, Old Politics: America's Military Procurement Muddle.* Washington, DC: Brookings Institution, 1989.
Brian Mitchell	*Weak Link: The Feminization of the American Military.* Washington, DC: Regnery Gateway, 1989.
Robert L. Pfaltzgraff Jr. and Jacquelyn K. Davis	*National Security Decisions: The Participants Speak.* Lexington, MA: D.C. Heath, 1990.
Leo Reddy and David Jones	*Burden Sharing: The Wrong Issue.* Washington, DC: Center for Strategic and International Studies, 1989.
Helen Rogan	*Mixed Company: Women in the Modern Army.* New York: G.P. Putnam's Sons, 1981.
Michael Rustad	*Women in Khaki: The American Enlisted Woman.* New York: Praeger, 1982.
Scott D. Sagan	*Moving Targets: Nuclear Strategy and National Security.* Princeton, NJ: Princeton University Press for Council on Foreign Relations, 1989.
Shelley Saywell	*Women in War.* New York: Viking Press, 1985.
Dorothy and Carl J. Schneider	*Sound Off! American Military Women Speak Out.* New York: E.P. Dutton, 1988.
Marc W. Smyrl	*Conflict or Codetermination? Congress, the President, and the Power to Make War.* Cambridge, MA: Ballinger Publishing Company, 1988.
Judith Hicks Stiehm	*Arms and the Enlisted Woman.* Philadelphia: Temple University Press, 1989.
John Stockwell	*The Praetorian Guard: The U.S. in the New International Security State.* Boston: South End Press, 1990.
Robert F. Turner	*The War Powers Resolution: Its Implementation in Theory and Practice.* Philadelphia: Foreign Policy Research Institute, 1983.
A.J. Vacevich et al.	*American Military Policy in Small Wars: The Case of El Salvador.* Washington, DC: Pergamon-Brassey's, 1988.
Murray Weidenbaum	*Military Spending and the Myth of Global Overstretch.* Washington, DC: Center for Strategic and International Studies, 1989.

Index

is wasteful, 122-127
  con, 128-133
democracy
  U.S. military promotes, 22, 48, 143
    con, 18, 55, 58-60
  in Eastern Europe, 32-33, 36, 56
    con, 151
Denmark, 41
détente, 170
deterrence
  conventional forces and, 143, 144,
    145
  nuclear weapons provide, 35, 57,
    74, 106, 108, 166, 168
    con, 52, 100, 157, 159, 170, 171-
    172
division air defense gun (DIVAD),
  126
Dole, Robert, 18
Dominican Republic, 59
drug trafficking, 24, 142, 144

Eastern Europe, 148
  democracy in, 22, 32-33, 36, 56,
    151
  revolutions of 1989, 27
    allow U.S. defense reductions, 35,
    150-151, 154, 170, 172
      con, 107, 109, 141, 143, 166
    call for U.S. involvement, 32-33,
    34, 36
      con, 29, 41-42
    U.S. strength helped promote,
    105-106
  Soviet troop withdrawals from, 27,
    35, 41, 108, 154, 170
  U.S. aid to, 112, 113
  U.S. trade with, 103
Ecuador, 59
Egypt, 144
Eisenhower, Dwight D., 148
El Salvador, 55, 60
Europe
  nuclear weapons in, 35-36, 40, 99
  Soviet threat to, 35, 39, 42
    has declined, 41, 44, 154
    has disappeared, 27, 28-29, 100,
    120, 150-151, 171-172
      con, 21, 107
  U.S. defense of, 148, 152
    cost of, 25, 155
    remains necessary, 20-21, 31-37
      con, 27-28, 29-30, 38-45, 100-101,
      149
    should be reduced, 26, 99, 153

con, 141, 144
weapons production, 28, 130-131
European Community, 34, 44
Ewing, Linda, 71

Faux, Jeff, 97
Feder, Don, 84
Fiscarelli, Rosemary, 38, 149
Fitzwater, Marlin, 162
FMC, Inc., 131
Ford, Gerald R., 148
foreign aid, 20, 112, 113-114
foreign policy, 47, 53, 55
forward deployment strategy, 24, 27,
  29, 30
France, 20, 28, 41, 44
French Revolution, 32
Friedman, Milton and Rose, 118

Galvin, John, 41
Gamble, Ed, 50, 106
Gansler, Jacques, 132-133
Garthoff, Raymond, 172
Gavin, James, 107
General Dynamics Corporation, 125
Germany, 28, 44
  economy, 20
  military forces, 41, 131
  NATO forces in, 34, 42, 43
  reunification of, 27, 98
    fears of aggression by, 21, 29-30,
    100
Gilbert, F. Charles, 165
Gilder, George, 68, 70
global protection against limited
  strikes (GPALS), 160
Gorbachev, Mikhail S., 107, 148, 149,
  158, 170
  political reforms, 33, 101, 108, 172
  Third World and, 47, 51, 58
  troop reductions, 41, 100, 150-151,
    153, 154
  U.S. aid to, 155
Great Britain, 20, 28, 42, 76
Greece, 59
Grumman Aircraft, 125
Guardian, 113
Guatemala, 55, 59, 60
guerrilla warfare, 68

Hispanic-Americans, 73
Hitler, Adolf, 18
human rights, 55, 60, 143, 151
Hun Sen, 47, 55
Hunter, Robert E., 33

189

191